LOUIS NOWRA was born in Melbourne. His plays include *Inner Voices*, *Visions*, *Inside the Island*, *The Golden Age*, *Capricornia*, *Byzantine Flowers*, *Summer of the Aliens*, *Così*, *Radiance*, *The Temple*, *Crow*, *The Incorruptible*, *The Jungle* and *The Language of the Gods*. He has written five non-fiction works, *The Cheated*, *Warne's World*, *Walkabout*, *Chihuahuas*, *Women and Me* and *Bad Dreaming*; the novels *The Misery of Beauty*, *Palu*, *Red Nights*, *Abaza*; and the memoirs *The Twelfth of Never* and *Shooting the Moon*. Some of his radio plays include *Albert Names Edward*, *The Song Room*, *Sydney* and *The Divine Hammer*. He has written the telemovies *Displaced Persons*, *Hunger* and *The Lizard King*. His screen credits include *Map of the Human Heart*, *Così*, *Heaven's Burning*, *The Matchmaker*, *Radiance*, *K-19: The Widowmaker* and *Black and White*. He lives in Sydney with his wife, Mandy Sayer.

LOUIS NOWRA

THE BOYCE TRILOGY

THE WOMAN WITH DOG'S EYES
THE MARVELLOUS BOY
THE EMPEROR OF SYDNEY

Currency Press, Sydney

CURRENCY PLAYS

First published in 2007
by Currency Press Pty Ltd,
PO Box 2287, Strawberry Hills, NSW, 2012, Australia
enquiries@currency.com.au
www.currency.com.au

NATIONAL LIBRARY OF AUSTRALIA CIP DATA
Louis Nowra, 1950-
The Boyce trilogy.
ISBN 978 0 86819 798 2 (pbk).
1. Boyce family (Fictitious characters) - Drama. 2. Family - Drama. I. Nowra, Louis, 1950- Woman with dog's eyes. II. Nowra, Louis, 1950- Marvellous boy. III. Nowra, Louis, 1950- Emperor of Sydney. IV. Title.
A822.4

  Publication of this title was assisted by the Commonwealth Government through the Australia Council, its arts funding and advisory body.

Set by Dean Nottle.
Printed by Ligare, Riverwood, NSW.
Cover design by Kate Florance, Currency Press.
The front cover shows Toby Schmitz as Luke Boyce in the Griffin Theatre Company production of *The Marvellous Boy*, 2005. (Photo: Michael Corridore)

Contents

vii THE GHOST IN THE MACHINE
       David Berthold

1   THE WOMAN WITH DOG'S EYES

55   THE MARVELLOUS BOY

117   THE EMPEROR OF SYDNEY

For Mandy
and
David Berthold

The Ghost in the Machine

Louis Nowra's Intimate Epic

One of the first things I did when I was appointed Artistic Director of Griffin Theatre Company in August 2003 was to call Louis Nowra. I had directed a few of Louis' plays for Sydney Theatre Company, and had always admired his work and enjoyed his company. More particularly, I knew that even though he lived just around the corner from Griffin's home at the SBW Stables Theatre in Kings Cross, and even though he was one of the Cross's most well-known and active literary identities (he had even co-edited a literary anthology of the Cross with his wife Mandy Sayer), Louis had never had one of his plays performed at what was his local theatre.

Louis pitched a play called *The Woman with Dog's Eyes*. I liked the title. Its Homeric origins were playful and its suggestion of Faulkner's *As I Lay Dying* was evocative. Louis was, I must say, somewhat sketchy on the detail, but the story seemed intriguing and right for the space. I programmed the play even though Louis hadn't written a word, a small detail that managed to escape detection. Every Artistic Director takes that kind of calculated risk at some point, though few admit it. But I did want to make a splash in my first season, and risk and reward are close friends.

Louis was considering a trilogy at this point, but kept that to himself. After all, *Dog's Eyes* might not take off. He needn't have worried: the production sold almost every ticket. *The Marvellous Boy* and *The Emperor of Sydney* followed successfully in successive years, and together these three plays formed one of the main dishes of my three seasons as Artistic Director.

The project gave us all a great deal of pleasure. Nicholas Dare (set and costumes) and Matthew Marshall (lighting) designed all three productions, and the actors remained committed to their characters throughout, with Toby Schmitz playing Luke Boyce in all three plays.

This continuity is a rare thing in theatre, and I'm sure it contributed greatly to the trilogy's considerable success at the box office.

The trilogy has a deliberate rhythm. The first play is set in one room in real time; the second opens out quite colourfully, moving outside of the family and across time and space; the third returns to the Racine-like focus of the first. The middle play sits in the more familiar Nowra territory, especially through the characters of Ray and Victor, who have cousins in other Nowra plays, while the one-room, real-time plays are unusual for this writer. It was, in part, an attempt to exploit the particular intimacy of Griffin's 120-seat theatre. It's a pressure cooker space, and Louis was keen to adjust his natural dramaturgy to capitalise on it in a way that was, for him at least, an experiment.

I'd love to see the trilogy played in one go, in repertory across a season and occasionally on one day. I think its rhythm would then be more evident and more enjoyable. I'd also be fascinated to follow Luke Boyce though the three plays, back-to-back. In one sense, the trilogy charts the journey of a young man from detachment to love to liberation. It's a great role, and seeing it play out from beginning to end would be enthralling. The plays are completely self-contained—Louis worked hard at this—but the experience of the full suite would, I believe, be something more than the sum of its parts.

Each of the three plays is a kind of ghost story. Here's how Louis describes the beginnings of *The Woman with Dog's Eyes*:

> The genesis of *The Woman with Dog's Eyes* can be traced back to the several times I stayed at hotels like the Carrington and Hydro-Majestic in the Blue Mountains. The most vivid occasion was during the Winter Solstice festival several years ago. My wife and I met a couple who had returned to the Hotel Carrington to celebrate their fortieth wedding anniversary. The husband was a man who was used to getting his way. His wife seemed brow beaten but, although she acted as if she were, I wondered just how weak she really was. On the night of the Winter Solstice there were firecrackers outside and a dinner and swing band inside. It had the feeling of another era as if the ghosts of the past and the contemporary hotel guests intermingled for a brief few hours.

This feeling is one shared by the characters of the play, particularly Luke, who is haunted by the idea that the hotel room they occupy has seen thousands of couples making love and fighting. A painting of the original owner of the hotel, a property-developing antecedent of Malcolm's, comes to life for Penny. That the events of the play occur on the winter solstice lends a celestial tension to this enchanted evening, particularly for Penny, who, like Gillian in the final play, believes in the observations of astrology.

Malcolm claims the power to haunt. He declares to his three sons that they cannot escape him, even after his death. For Malcolm, his soul is his genes, and so his soul is forever inside his sons. Over three plays, Luke will fight against being thus possessed by his father.

The ghost story of *The Marvellous Boy* is of a different quality. Louis has a remarkable ability to take significant elements of true events and to transform them into something indisputably his fiction, so that they become ghosts in the machine. It went unremarked upon in the media, though not in the foyer, that *The Woman with Dog's Eyes* was inspired by events that traumatised Sydney's Moran family, details of which were aired in a million-dollar court case. I remember being at a performance at which a lawyer's jaw dropped as the production unfolded. She was personally involved with the Moran case and saw in the play a corollary that shocked her in its insight and audacity. She claimed to know *exactly* how the trilogy would end. She was wrong.

The Marvellous Boy draws on different real-life Sydney stories. Here's how Louis describes the genesis of this second play:

> Only after finishing the play did I recognise some of the other sources for *The Marvellous Boy*. Once when I was living in Kings Cross I lived next door to an ornate Victorian terrace. I became intrigued by a man in his thirties who regularly visited a woman in her early fifties. It turned out that the younger man was her lover and she had been his father's mistress. I had also heard stories about Juanita Neilson, the heiress who was murdered when she tried to stop developers ruining Kings Cross. Yet *The Marvellous Boy* only faintly resembles her story—it was just something that became one of the many strands of the story, as much as caviar and parrots are also strands to it. The over riding feature of the

play is really how one of the sons from the first play, Luke, believes he is in control of his life and can determine his own destiny when everyone around him, including the woman he loves, knows more than he does.

The disappearance and presumed murder of Juanita Nielson is one of Australia's great unsolved crimes, a standout badge of 1970s Sydney, and an iconic Kings Cross story. But in *The Marvellous Boy* it has become a ghost. Jim Anderson, the 'Iago of Kings Cross' and business partner of the late Abe Saffron, is reflected in Ray. Anderson was closely linked with suspicious fires, and he did die of bird flu. Frank Theeman, property developer and founder of the Osti fashion empire, similarly inhabits parts of Malcolm. It is testament to Louis' ability to transform and own his sources that Malcolm Boyce, over the first two plays, can suggest identities as distinct in time and place as Doug Moran and Frank Theeman, yet be completely himself. There is something elegiac about this part of the story—and it is just a small part—yet it is one that tells us more than we might care to know about how some quite contemporary Sydney families, businesses and lives are run.

In the final moments of *The Marvellous Boy*, we see what might be a real ghost. Malcolm's genetic victory appears complete—the son has fallen in love with his father's mistress, after all—and Luke experiences an epileptic seizure. Out of the electrical haze that follows, he sees his beloved Esther. It's a breathtaking moment, a vision of love beyond death.

The Emperor of Sydney unfolds in an antechamber to death. Misbehaving air conditioning chills the room, and the model of the 'Boyce' development is electrically faulty. Malcolm will speak beyond the confines of his deathbed. When Louis and I began talking about the question of how we might deal with 'Malcolm's Voice' as it then appeared simply on the page, we agreed that a bold solution would be to have the sons speak these lines. In this way, Malcolm was literally possessing his sons in a way familiar to us from horror films. Thematically, this seemed to us the logical extension of where this aspect of the trilogy was heading, and theatrically, it had the potential to be surprising and compelling. And so it proved. It was thrilling to watch Toby Schmitz, Jack Finsterer and Alex Dimitriades channel Danny Adcock in ways that were precise, revealing and spirited. They were able to do so because they had been there from the beginning.

When Malcolm finally dies, these voices stop, and we are left to wonder how Malcolm will continue to haunt. Todd speaks of feeling an electric charge when he grasped his dying father's hand, and we feel that somehow Malcolm has found a habitat inside his troubled son. Thus strengthened, Todd takes control of the family empire: the 'weakest' wins (or so he sees it), just as the 'weak' Penny made an astonishing victory in the first play, as the snow fell and the fireworks flared.

The trilogy, I think, asks a lot of difficult questions. Is it possible to escape the genetic influence of our parents? Malcolm and Diane both claim to have done so, and Luke may well have achieved the same. How does 'madness' operate within families and marriages? How do the weak win? What is the value and cost of empire? How does one move from emotional detachment to irresistible and redefining love? In some ways, these are familiar, Nowraesque concerns. Madness, the displaced and the dysfunctional all operate in the texture of these plays just as they have from the very beginnings of this writer's journey. In Victor, for example, we see a figure that forms part of a genetic strand stretching back to Louis' first play, *Albert Names Edward* (1975), and through probably a dozen or more since. Dynastic families, with their attendant illnesses, are also familiar terrain, as is the desire for empire.

The trilogy, while traversing these distinctive concerns, most movingly lays bare a young man's fight for the right to be himself, and the right to love. This is an intimate epic, one that argues for the weak over the strong, empathy over detachment and love over vanity. In its closing moment, our marvellous boy speaks gently to his father, and forgives. As a light is switched off, a young man is set free, and all is possible.

David Berthold
March 2007

DAVID BERTHOLD was the Artistic Director of Griffin Theatre Company 2003-06, and directed the premiere productions of all three plays in The Boyce Trilogy.

THE WOMAN WITH DOG'S EYES

Danny Adcock (foreground) as Malcolm and Alex Dimitriades as Todd in the 2004 Griffin Theatre Company production of THE WOMAN WITH DOG'S EYES. *(Photo: Robert McFarlane)*

FIRST PERFORMANCE

The Woman with Dog's Eyes was first produced by Griffin Theatre
Company at the SBW Stables, Sydney, on 1 October 2004 with the
following cast:

MALCOLM	Danny Adcock
PENNY	Jane Harders
LUKE	Toby Schmitz
KEITH	Jack Finsterer
TODD	Alex Dimitriades

Director, David Berthold
Designer, Nicholas Dare
Lighting Designer, Matthew Marshall

CHARACTERS

MALCOLM BOYCE
PENNY BOYCE, his wife
KEITH BOYCE, oldest son
TODD BOYCE, middle son
LUKE BOYCE, youngest son

SETTING

The Blue Mountains. An enormous room in an old Edwardian era hotel. It has recently been renovated in its original style. Time: now.

An enormous room in an old Edwardian-era hotel. It has recently been renovated in its original style. Night. MALCOLM BOYCE, *a man in his sixties, wearing tuxedo trousers and white shirt but no bow tie or jacket, enters with a glass and a tiny bottle of whisky from the mini bar.*

MALCOLM: It's like the lunatics have taken over the asylum. Where do they get them? Maybe they're all inbred. Not enough oxygen in the mountain air... starved of it at birth. [*On to another subject*] Can't he ever be on time? He's never been on time. [*Looking at the bottle*] Measly. Everything here—measly. Little people. Tiny people. Drongos... [*On to another subject*] Just like that—coming at you... when you don't expect it. Like a freight train. Jesus... so unfair. [*Starting to pour the whisky into the glass slowly, as if staring at every single drop*] Drop, drop, drop. Wringing it out, bit by bit. Drop, drop, plop, plop...

His wife, PENNY, *comes out of the bathroom wearing a gorgeous frock, but has yet to fully apply make-up, necklace and earrings.*

PENNY: I thought there was someone else in the room. Sign of madness, you know.

MALCOLM: What is it with hotels and mini bottles? You'd think all hotels were preparing for a conference of dwarfs. [*Sniffing it*] And cheap at that.

PENNY: Malcolm. [*She indicates he zip up the back of her dress.*] I thought you'd rung room service?

MALCOLM: [*doing up the zip*] Half an hour ago.

PENNY: It seems like a really big deal for them—maybe they're all pre-occupied preparing the dinner and fireworks. [*Looking at a photograph on the wall*] He has sad eyes. [*He's zipped her up.*] Thank you.

MALCOLM: Who?

PENNY: The man in the photograph. He must have been the original owner. Men from that period always wore beards or florid moustaches. It must have made them look funny.

MALCOLM: He doesn't look funny.

PENNY: When they were naked. All bushy. Women's skin must have been rubbed raw when they kissed. Is there one for me?

He motions to the far end of the room.

MALCOLM: Took me forever to find the mini bar, it's in the wardrobe.

She goes offstage to get herself a drink.

Should you be having one?

PENNY: [*offstage*] It's a party. Our party.

MALCOLM: You noticed the staff here? If they're not mouth-breathers they drag their knuckles across the ground when they walk. Is Luke here?

PENNY: [*offstage*] Yes.

MALCOLM: When?

PENNY: [*offstage*] Reception told me he signed in an hour ago.

MALCOLM: Why didn't you tell me?

PENNY: [*offstage*] You didn't ask.

MALCOLM: I asked dozens of times.

PENNY: [*offstage*] This afternoon.

MALCOLM: What sort of logic's that?

She returns with a glass of whisky.

PENNY: Maybe they don't want people to use it.

MALCOLM: Use what?

PENNY: The mini bar—that's why they hide it. [*Holding out her glass*] Cheers. To us.

They clink glasses.

MALCOLM: Just go easy, that's all.

PENNY *sips and then looks out the window.*

PENNY: It's so still. Everything goes silent before snow falls. Like a hush. I wonder if those people really believe in fairies?

MALCOLM: Who?

PENNY: Those women dressed as fairies.

MALCOLM: Didn't see them. There were enough whackos to look at anyway.

PENNY: They had a fairy stall. All those sculptures and fairy toys. I used to believe in them when I was a little girl. They had to have a wand. I pulled two of my teeth out on purpose so the tooth fairy would come. Jiggled them back and forth for hours. Mum said, 'You are such a lucky girl, Penny'. I didn't tell her, of course.

MALCOLM: Well, the people up here believe in anything. I guess being on the dole gives you time to believe in all that stuff. [*He looks at an opened magazine—the astrology page.*] What are you again? Aries. [*Reading*] 'Later this week Mercury stations directly in your sign. Because it does so in the aspect of potent Pluto, what might ordinarily be a psychological process is really a spiritual one. The difference is the extent to which you feel compelled to consider the deeper implications of your decisions. Yet there's another factor involved, which is aligning your mind with your sense of beauty and value. You're more sensitive than you give yourself credit for, particularly now. That sensitivity is calling you towards greater awareness. There are better things than certainty. And beware of putting people under your sensitised gaze. Your know more than they do and they know. Be gentle. You don't want to chew this person 'til the flavour's gone.' [*Pause.*] You don't want to chew this person until the flavour's gone. Well, that's an insight.

PENNY: You don't have to believe in it.

MALCOLM: Why do you read it, for God's sake? It's stupid.

Pause.

PENNY: Clear sky. That blue ring around the moon—they say it's going to snow.

MALCOLM: I hope *they* isn't the staff—

PENNY: What have you got against them? It's only been re-opened for a couple of months. They've probably got teething problems.

MALCOLM: They'd get lost in a revolving door.

PENNY: Pay no attention to them.

MALCOLM: I have to deal with them.

PENNY: No, you don't. Forget them.

MALCOLM: [*sarcastically*] Puff, they're gone.

Silence. PENNY *walks around the room, curious.*

PENNY: His eyes follow you about. [*Pause.*] When are the fireworks?

MALCOLM: Plenty of time.

PENNY: Fireworks always make people happy.

MALCOLM: No doubt the hotel will give the job to a halfwit who's afraid of matches. Why does Luke have this damn thing about time.

PENNY: He's always been like that. You know that. Why are you so…?

MALCOLM: So what?

PENNY: Toey.

MALCOLM: What are you on about?

Pause.

PENNY: I want… I want things to go well. [*Looking at the photograph*] Maybe he spent so much money on the hotel… that's why he's sad. It would have looked glorious when it opened. [*Re: her frock*] Is this right for tonight?

MALCOLM: Sure.

PENNY: I brought that other one… the turquoise.

MALCOLM: It's perfect.

PENNY: It was the colour I wore at our reception. Matched my eyes, Mum said. It was her way of giving a compliment.

A knock on the door.

MALCOLM: About time. It's open!

LUKE *their son, late twenties, enters. He is wearing a tuxedo shirt and trousers, but no bow tie and jacket.*

LUKE: You look disappointed.

PENNY: Your father was expecting room service.

LUKE: Your room's much bigger than mine.

PENNY: We're the ones having the anniversary.

LUKE: There was this dying man and he was gasping pitifully to his wife. 'Give me one last request, Jane,' he pleads. 'Of course, Bill,' she said softly. 'Six months after I die,' he says, 'I want you to marry Joe'. 'But I thought you hated Joe,' she says. With his last breath, he replies, 'I do'.

PENNY: Thank you for your gift of humour.

LUKE: [*regarding the room*] They did a great renovation.

MALCOLM: Must have cost a pretty penny.

LUKE: The Edwardian era was fussy, wasn't it?

PENNY: It was a human era to live in.

LUKE: Even the ceiling's been really worked over.

PENNY: Not all people want to live in white boxes with metal furniture.

MALCOLM: Why weren't you at lunch?

LUKE: I was still back in Sydney.

MALCOLM: We said lunch.

LUKE: I phoned and left a message. You had Keith, didn't you?
MALCOLM: Where's your bow tie?
LUKE: Back in my room.
MALCOLM: You have to be properly dressed. It's for your mother.
LUKE: I think I've got a bit of time.
PENNY: And don't forget your coat—it's cold outside.
LUKE: Did you see the parade?
PENNY: It was after lunch. Lots of women dressed in purple with witches' hats and men pretending to be goblins or leprechauns.
LUKE: But why do they have it?
PENNY: It's winter solstice. [*Noticing he doesn't know the term*] When the sun is the farthest distance from the celestial equator—when it enters the sign of Cancer.
MALCOLM: Oh, God, not more astrology—
LUKE: You don't think they should get a life?
MALCOLM: Most of the women here are pregnant. Single mums. All on welfare. When we first came here only the wealthy could afford to be here. Now all these losers come up here and bludge off the welfare system for the rest of their lives. Hippy paradise.
PENNY: And there were a lot of little bells. They like bells. And stalls.
MALCOLM: Crystals and vegetarian food. Why do vegetarians always look so pale and unhealthy?
PENNY: It was nice.
LUKE: Get your palm read at the stalls?
MALCOLM: Tarot.
LUKE: [*to* PENNY] What does the future foretell?
MALCOLM: You don't want to chew this person until the flavour's gone.
LUKE: Rather cannibalistic.
MALCOLM: I'm going downstairs to get the whisky.

MALCOLM *exits.*

PENNY: He was making fun of the astrology thing... He always makes fun of what I believe in.
LUKE: He seems a bit—
PENNY: Toey. Did you bring Todd?
LUKE: Yeah. Do you think you should be doing this?
PENNY: Now or never. It's our fortieth. This is the time to do it.
LUKE: It's your funeral.

PENNY: I was hoping we could have done it at lunch. It would have been so much easier to have done it over lunch. In a public place.

LUKE: I got there and he didn't want to come. It took me a while to convince him.

PENNY: Why? What was the problem?

LUKE: Frightened, of course.

PENNY: But that's what he wanted. It's what we both want. At least he's here. His girlfriend is nice, isn't she?

LUKE: I didn't meet her.

PENNY: Isn't she here with him?

LUKE: No.

PENNY: Oh, dear. I thought with her here it would soften everything. She's no intellectual, but she's clever. They'll make a good couple. [*Re: something on his tuxedo*] Spot. Where is he?

She cleans off the spot herself.

LUKE: I put him on the first floor. I thought he wouldn't run into Dad that way.

PENNY: Did you tell Keith?

LUKE: Haven't seen him yet. Is his missus here?

PENNY: He says she's in a health farm.

LUKE: Sounds like another breakdown.

PENNY: She used to have such bright eyes. Did you bring April?

He shrugs.

Luke, she was lovely. I had high hopes for the both of you.

LUKE: I wanted a girl with a name later in the year. June, July.

PENNY: She loved you. And I thought you loved her.

LUKE: I didn't like the sensation. It was sort of like falling from a highwire hoping there was a net but there didn't seem to be one.

PENNY: That's being in love.

LUKE: It's an awful feeling because you want the intensity to end and then you're afraid it will. Anyway, it decided me on the woman I wanted. She has to be after my money. And particularly gorgeous. When we're married she has to spend all the time with ladies who lunch. A marriage without those dreadful illusions. And she has to be very good at faking orgasms. [*A beat.*] They always sound much better than real ones.

PENNY: I know you don't mean it, but then I never know what you mean. April must have hurt you.

LUKE: No, I hurt her. Is this the room where you spent your honeymoon?

PENNY: It was really dingy then. The hotel was. Had discoloured walls. Well, not the walls themselves but the wallpaper. Everyone smoked in those days. Because I was a waitress here they gave me and your father the best room—for a discount.

LUKE: I thought you were a nurse.

PENNY: Your father made me give it up. He couldn't stand the fact that I'd be handling men's private parts.

LUKE: Is that the same bed?

PENNY: Oh, goodness no. It was on its last legs even then.

LUKE: I often wonder, when I'm in motels, hotels, about the couples who've been there before me. I look at the bed and think—how many couples have made love in it? Fought. Committed adultery. Lost their virginity. Couldn't do it. Died, even. So many ghosts. This place must be about a hundred years old, wouldn't you say? So a couple every weekend—that makes five thousand crying, moaning, laughing, shouting, ecstatic, silent, hating couples have been in this room.

PENNY: That head of yours.

LUKE: You know what kind it is.

PENNY: Are you looking after yourself?

LUKE: Yes, I have every intention of cutting open my skull, taking out my brain and put it under a running tap to wash out all that muck. [*Motioning to the photograph*] Who's that?

PENNY: We think it's the original owner. You know, I'm really pleased that Malcolm never had a moustache or beard. They make men look secretive. And a bit ridiculous—when they're naked.

Noise and colour of a solitary sky rocket outside the window.

LUKE: They've started already.

PENNY: Your dad would kill them if they did. He's got his heart set on the firecrackers.

A knock on the door.

Yes.

KEITH *enters, late thirties, wearing a tuxedo and everything except a bow tie. He is carrying a bottle of whisky.*

KEITH: Some guy from room service left this. Obviously he got Dad's room number and our names mixed up. [*To* LUKE] Glad you could make it.

LUKE: My penis reduction operation took longer than expected.

KEITH: I had to put up with Dad whingeing all through lunch: 'Where's Luke? Where's Luke?'

PENNY: He wasn't whingeing.

KEITH: He was annoyed that Luke wasn't there, like it was my fault.

PENNY: Luke was picking up Todd.

KEITH: What do you mean?

LUKE: He's here. Under our feet as we speak.

KEITH: I don't get it.

PENNY: He's going to be with us for dinner.

KEITH: Have you told Dad?

PENNY: No. And leave it to me. I'll pick the moment.

KEITH: He's going to hit the roof. When are you going to do it? How you going to do it?

LUKE: We're going to present him with a giant birthday cake and Todd's going to jump out of it.

KEITH: You're stupid.

PENNY: Don't call me stupid.

KEITH: He just did that magazine interview. He mentioned all of us except Todd. As far as Dad's concerned he's dead.

The door opens and MALCOLM *enters.*

LUKE: Hey, we were just talking about you.

MALCOLM: The concierge said he had delivered the—

KEITH: [*holding out his bottle*] To my room.

MALCOLM: [*taking the bottle*] Maybe lobotomies are very cheap up here. You see that sky rocket? I'm down there and go outside and one of the local clowns said he was going to test one. I said, 'Shouldn't you hold it away from you?' It nearly took off his face. Probably would have been an improvement. Never seen so many pimples on a kid. So much for the healthy climate up here, they keep on bragging about.

He holds out the bottle. Both sons nod, wanting a drink.

And what were you talking about?

LUKE: How much in love with Mum you must be after forty years.

MALCOLM: It's freezing out there. Wear your coats for the crackers.

KEITH: Why can't we watch them from inside?

MALCOLM: It's our wedding anniversary, so for the first time in your life—obey us.

LUKE: [*to* KEITH] This is the room where you were conceived.

KEITH: This?

LUKE: [*to* PENNY] Wasn't it?

She nods.

[*To* KEITH] Bring back any early memories?

KEITH: The hope I wouldn't have a brother like you.

LUKE *raises his glass,* KEITH *follows.*

LUKE: To Mum and Dad.

KEITH: To Mum and Dad.

MALCOLM: You bring any girl?

LUKE *shakes his head.*

There's a swing band after dinner. The best in the state. Who are you going to dance with?

LUKE: [*to* KEITH] I'll lead.

KEITH: [*to* MALCOLM] I phoned Sydney and arranged for you to get a new secretary.

PENNY: What happened to Christine?

MALCOLM: She was always sullen.

LUKE: That's the trouble with ugly women, they always bring their problems to work. Beautiful women don't.

PENNY: Luke.

LUKE: It's true. She could never get a man. She should have become lesbian. Lesbianism gives a plain girl a chance to find some happiness in life.

KEITH: When do you stop?

LUKE: I'm on a roll.

KEITH: I've also been on the phone to some members of the Board—

PENNY: It's Saturday! This is our anniversary. Stop talking about work.

MALCOLM: Never say that. I've told you before.

Pause.

PENNY: This is a special occasion.

MALCOLM: Never interfere.

PENNY: Lips are sealed. Brain zipped up. Naughty Penny.

Silence.

I'll finish my make-up.

*She pours herself some whisky with a sense of defiance. Silence.
She goes into the bathroom.*

KEITH: Great. She's going to get sloshed.

MALCOLM: So what's the gist of what they said?

KEITH: Immigration looks like doing a raid on the Greenpastures project.

MALCOLM: How many illegals do we have?

KEITH: About twenty per cent. Without them, we'd be way behind.

MALCOLM: We'll have to pull most of them out until after the raid.

KEITH: We could sacrifice about two dozen.

MALCOLM: Why is the government like this? Those illegals work fucking hard. Jesus, try and get Anglos to work as hard. Those Chinese and Indonesians work their arses off.

LUKE: And besides, they're midgets—which would explain why all our apartment blocks have low ceilings.

MALCOLM: You have any better suggestions? Those idiots in Canberra yell and scream saying they're taking the jobs of Australians. Name one fucking Australian whose job they've taken.

LUKE: I agree. I truly do.

MALCOLM: Let's try and do a deal with Immigration.

KEITH: They're illegals.

MALCOLM: The law is inflexible, but money makes it elastic.

KEITH: I'm not bribing them.

MALCOLM: I give money to both parties—

KEITH: If you didn't, we'd be raided more often.

MALCOLM: This world… this world is crazy. People who want to work are jumped upon and laziness seen as a virtue. [*To* KEITH] And what about the State Government, why in the hell are they sitting on the sidelines with the Hesperus Park thing?

KEITH: The press.

MALCOLM: Why's the PR going so wrong? I did that long magazine interview. [*To* KEITH] You explained our designs very well—

LUKE: They hate us.

MALCOLM: Who?

KEITH: Up-market newspapers... you know, trendies.

MALCOLM: Why do those people always whinge about new things?

KEITH: They just think of us as cheap.

MALCOLM: We do affordable housing. That's the fucking thing that gets me. Those fucking people despise people who can't afford palaces. Anyway, this Hesperus thing is different. We got that architect. It's for those trendies who are bitching about us all the time.

KEITH: It's the area.

MALCOLM: It's swamplands.

KEITH: With birds and kangaroos.

MALCOLM: What the world needs now is more kangaroos. We're keeping half the grasslands, most of the birdlife will stay. The experts say that.

LUKE: Not the newspapers' experts.

MALCOLM: We paid a fortune for that advice.

KEITH: As far as the public are now concerned we're going to bulldoze the lot, instead of only building on a quarter of the park. They've formed this local committee who've got good PR.

MALCOLM: It's not a committee. It's someone else who wants to build there. You fucking get them, Keith. Get some money together and form another committee for the project. We'll buy off the locals how the others did. You get paid ads, you get some of those MPs on our side—they owe us big. This is unfair. For fucking years we have been looked down upon, and now we're doing something special they come at us. I would just like to get in a room with that scum—

LUKE: Or as you said in that interview: 'I'm a good hater, I admit it.' That's not good PR, Dad.

MALCOLM: It's the truth. Everything I said in that interview is the truth. You know why we're not liked?

LUKE: We're considered nouveau riche.

MALCOLM: But you've both been to university.

KEITH: We're associated with cheap housing.

MALCOLM: Warmer. You see, we saved The Beauchamp. No one else could afford to restore it, let alone live in it. It's always in magazines. And yet we're still considered... you know, not quite the right stuff. But do you know the reason? People think this country's classless. It fucking isn't. Everyone looks up to old money, old families, as if they're the fucking apex. Our name isn't old, it isn't famous. But it will be and the next generation, you watch... we'll be considered like them. So you two start putting your dicks into the right girls.

KEITH: I appreciate the advice.

LUKE: Couldn't have put it better myself.

MALCOLM: Time is of the essence, Keith. This is our biggest project.

KEITH: That's the problem.

MALCOLM: It's no problem we can't beat. From the beginning I've had people put obstacles in my way. You boys don't know the half of it—

KEITH: I'm not talking about that.

MALCOLM: What else is there to talk about?

KEITH: The money for Hesperus—

MALCOLM: It's not going to be called Hesperus Park anymore either. It's going to be called Boyce.

LUKE: If you name it after us, we're going to get slaughtered in the press.

MALCOLM: We tell no one until we've got the go-ahead. And then, let me tell you Luke, people get used to anything. They'll be saying our name with pride.

KEITH: The problem is more simple than fucking naming it. It's not going to work.

MALCOLM: What in the hell are you talking about?

KEITH: We've only sold half of the estate. We're financially overstretched. We can't pay for the initial costs of Hesperus Park.

LUKE: We can borrow.

MALCOLM: We can borrow.

KEITH: All it needs is for there to be a slight downturn in the housing market and we're done for. That Hesperus thing will destroy us.

MALCOLM: Boyce.

KEITH: Well, Boyce will destroy us. It's commercial suicide.

Pause.

MALCOLM: You have a brilliant mind, Keith, but you lack balls.

KEITH: No, no, no. I have a sense of reality. Financial reality.

MALCOLM: If you don't risk, you get nowhere.

KEITH: This is not a risk—Hesperus Park is Russian roulette.

LUKE: So we put a gun to our head.

KEITH: Don't be fucking facetious.

MALCOLM: Luke has guts. He's like me—he knows risk is the name of the game.

KEITH: He likes risks because he doesn't care. If he lived in a caravan park tomorrow he wouldn't care.

LUKE: I most certainly would. Where would my butler live?

KEITH: You don't fucking care.

LUKE: Big brother, you don't know me. I don't want to be poor. I want money. After all, money is the root of all women.

KEITH: See, always with those cracks. I care about our business. I truly do.

MALCOLM: I know you do. So does Luke. I know we risk everything on Hesperus Park. But that's how I've always done it.

KEITH: Times are different.

LUKE: It's our biggest project. If we pull it off then it'll be our biggest achievement—

MALCOLM: Our monument. Boyce.

KEITH: I am not giving up on this. It's sheer madness. I'm on the Board— remember. Luke isn't.

MALCOLM: Are you threatening me?

KEITH: I am wanting you to see sense.

MALCOLM: I have all the sense I need. I'm going ahead with it. And when it's finished I won't expect an apology.

KEITH: Apology?

MALCOLM: You'll be proud to be a Boyce.

KEITH: I am.

MALCOLM: So get some balls.

KEITH *goes to say something.*

Enough! Just do what I say. Now how are the preparations going? What about the band?

KEITH: The Musicians Union said they were the best swing band in the country.

MALCOLM: Dinner?

LUKE: We're the only table that has been reserved. The other hotel guests will have to scramble for their seats. By the way, why do they call it the Crystal Ball?

MALCOLM: That's what they used to call them when your mum and me married.

LUKE: Why don't you tell her that you've organised it all. She'll love that.

MALCOLM: She'll fuss. She said that she wished this place still had a Crystal Ball—so I made it happen. Clicked my fingers and, hey presto.

KEITH: A click of the fingers and Hesperus Park will happen?

MALCOLM: Yes, like The Boyce will happen.

> KEITH *goes to say something when* MALCOLM *holds up his hand.* PENNY, *now with make-up on, comes out of the bathroom. She holds up her whisky glass. She's only drunk half, but seems a little vague.*

PENNY: [*holding up her glass*] See? Half. Now aren't I a good girl? What about the moon?

LUKE: Haven't looked.

PENNY: It affects the tides and the way people behave. [*To* MALCOLM] It stands to reason that stars will also have effects on humans too.

KEITH: For Christ sakes.

PENNY: What's your problem, Keith?

MALCOLM: Just go easy on things.

PENNY: I'm not criticising you. I'm not talking about the business. That would get me into trouble. I'm merely saying that if I believe in something, I have a right to believe in it.

MALCOLM: Just behave.

PENNY: In public? When haven't I? I want names. Places. Dates.

> *Silence.*

Your father was never as abrasive as you know him. Abrasive man, now. He didn't chew up people and throw them out.

MALCOLM: How long will this go on, Penny?

PENNY: He was a very romantic man. No wonder he didn't like me handling the private parts of other men.

MALCOLM: What are you talking about?

PENNY: I can talk about this. I know what I'm talking about with this. You were romantic. We got married in the registry office down the street. We had about a dozen friends. All except one were mine. He had one friend then. He was lonely.

MALCOLM: I wasn't lonely.

PENNY: And shy. So it took a lot of courage to do what he did during the wedding dinner downstairs. In the Grand Dining Room.

MALCOLM: I didn't do anything.

PENNY: Yes, you did. When you made the toast. You said you'd sing my favourite song. And you did. You stood up and sang it for me. I knew how much it took. You were so shy. It was very romantic. Everyone applauded and you went bright, bright red. Puce, really.

MALCOLM: Puce... [*To his sons*] Me, puce.

PENNY: It was such a romantic thing to do.

LUKE: What was the song?

MALCOLM *shrugs.*

PENNY: You jolly well know. 'Some Enchanted Evening'.

LUKE: [*amused*] 'Some Enchanted Evening'? You got up and sang that?

MALCOLM: I think I'd had a drink too many.

PENNY: You didn't drink then. You did it for me. My heart tingled. Before you were abrasive.

LUKE: Well, I'm impressed, Dad. Sing it now.

MALCOLM: Now?

LUKE: It's your fortieth. You're back here. All right then, sing it when we're down in the Grand Dining Room

MALCOLM: Why are you so smart-arsed?

LUKE: I think it was very romantic.

PENNY: There you go—romantic.

LUKE: How was his voice?

PENNY: It was the thought.

MALCOLM: See, that's why I'm not singing it.

PENNY: You didn't worry about being embarrassed then.

Pause.

KEITH: [*needling*] Yes, why don't you sing it?

MALCOLM: [*to* PENNY] Keith didn't get his way.

PENNY: Didn't you, Keith?

KEITH: I happen to be right and these two wrong.

PENNY: Please… you have to keep to what the tarot reader told me. Tonight is going to be beautiful.

MALCOLM: Your mother has booked in for a séance with that clown tomorrow.

LUKE: Upturned glass moving around touching letters of the alphabet?

PENNY: It works.

LUKE: Which dead person are you contacting?

PENNY: It's my secret.

MALCOLM: Her father.

PENNY: It's my secret, I said.

MALCOLM: Her dad couldn't do any wrong. The perfect man. She would have married him if she could have.

PENNY: He was a kind, gentle man. He had a wonderful laugh.

MALCOLM: Perhaps he was. How would I know? He was dead when I married you. [*To* LUKE] Be careful of marrying a woman whose father is dead. You're always going to be in competition with him.

PENNY: That's not true. You're so unlike him. There was no competition.

MALCOLM: Anyway, I believe in that kind of psychic stuff. So much so that it's going in my will.

LUKE: You?

MALCOLM: Yep. After I'm dead you two boys have to hold a séance every morning and contact me. I'll tell you what work you have to do for the rest of the day. That way I'll still be in control in the afterlife.

PENNY: You know, if you could, you would.

MALCOLM: I'll haunt you boys after death.

LUKE: You already do a good job now.

MALCOLM: [*holding out his glass to* LUKE] Top up.

PENNY: Put on your bow tie and jacket, darling.

> LUKE *goes to say something when his mother motions no and points to the floor. He knows what that means.*

LUKE: Plenty of time.

PENNY: Do it now. Bring me back a present.

LUKE: I'll be back soon.

MALCOLM: Where you going?

> LUKE *exits.*

Be back… when? [*To* PENNY] I thought you said he'd be a bit down 'cause of that girl?

PENNY: I was wrong. I think he's relieved he doesn't have to commit. [*To* KEITH] I can say I'm wrong. What's really wrong with Gillian?

KEITH: I told you at lunch.

PENNY: No, you didn't. You only said she couldn't come.

KEITH: She's in one of her downward spirals.

PENNY: How long will she be in there?

KEITH: The shrink says he doesn't know.

PENNY: You should have told me so I could visit her.

KEITH: I didn't want to spoil the anniversary.

PENNY: Maybe she could have come. You know, had a good time.

KEITH: She would have spoilt it. Either she'd be dancing on the tabletop or down in the dumps.

PENNY: That's okay to dance on tabletops.

KEITH: Drinking from a bottle with a finger up her fanny?

PENNY: Don't be silly.

KEITH: I live with her. I know her. I've seen her do it.

PENNY: Really? You never told me.

KEITH: I didn't think you'd like to know.

MALCOLM: What are you going to do about it?

KEITH: Like what?

MALCOLM: Divorce.

KEITH: It's difficult—

MALCOLM: She's mad, surely it would be easy.

PENNY: You can't.

MALCOLM: She's loony.

PENNY: That's why you can't. Wait until she's better. You can't cut her off now. You have to stand by her.

KEITH: Stand by what? Stand by who? The one who's dancing on tabletops, the one cutting her wrists?

PENNY: She wasn't always like that.

KEITH: That's what I mean. She's no longer that girl.

PENNY: Maybe you changed her.

KEITH: Maybe you're mixing your medication and drink.

MALCOLM: Hey, that's enough.

Silence.

KEITH: It's snowing.

PENNY: So it is. It looks like fairyland.

MALCOLM: See, Keith, I click my fingers and—snap, snow.

KEITH: I'll get changed.

PENNY: Don't forget your coat.

KEITH *exits.*

Fireworks in the snow. It's going to look gorgeous.

Pause.

MALCOLM: He can't help it if his wife's gone mad.

PENNY: You don't desert her when she's sick. You stand by her. [*Pause.*] She was a lovely girl.

MALCOLM: She still is.

PENNY: No. It's like all her insides have been scooped out.

MALCOLM: He wants to have a family. She won't give him one.

PENNY: It's her revenge for his coldness.

MALCOLM: How can you criticise him?

PENNY: Because he's always been cold if he doesn't get his way. Like you. Don't be defensive. I'm merely stating a fact. It's like you tell me that I'm too silly for words. And you're right, sometimes I can be too silly for words. [*Pause.*] Dah, dee, dah, dee, dah… [*Pause.*] Is the business in trouble?

MALCOLM: Jesus, Penny.

PENNY: You don't have to give me the details.

MALCOLM: It's fine. It's fine. Keith gets a bit wary at a time when he should be taking risks.

PENNY: Not everyone can be like you.

MALCOLM: I put him on the Board and he becomes a handbrake.

PENNY: It's nice to have a balance.

MALCOLM: See, too silly for words. [*Pause.*] I really don't have the time to put up with dissension inside my own family when there's enough enemies out there trying to stop this project going ahead. I just don't have the time, Penny.

A knock at the door.

Come in!

The door opens and LUKE *comes in, now dressed, followed by a wary* TODD, *wearing a cheap suit and carrying a coat.* MALCOLM *is startled to see him and not at all pleased.*

PENNY: [*kissing him*] Todd.

Silence.

TODD: Hi, Dad.

Silence.

MALCOLM: What are you doing here? [*To* PENNY] This is your work.

PENNY: This is our son.

Pause.

MALCOLM: You can go.

TODD: [*to* PENNY] I told you.

TODD *is about to go.*

PENNY: You're staying.

Silence as MALCOLM *pours himself a drink.*

MALCOLM: [*to* LUKE] You were in on it too.

LUKE: Hey, don't shoot the messenger.

MALCOLM: And don't you say anything, smart-arse. [*To* PENNY] Why did you want to ruin tonight?

PENNY: I have no intention of ruining it.

MALCOLM: Too fucking silly for words.

PENNY: Put me down... but I don't care, he's staying.

PENNY *goes to the mini bar to get a glass.*

MALCOLM: [*to* LUKE] You drove him up?

LUKE: Yeah.

MALCOLM: Got no car, has he? Why doesn't he steal one and smash it up?

PENNY: [*coming back with the glass*] He's going to get married.

She holds up the glass for TODD *who nods. She pours him a whisky.*

She's a nice girl.

MALCOLM: [*to* TODD] How did you get her, then?

PENNY: They're going to get married.

MALCOLM: You after some money?

TODD: No.

PENNY: No, he's not. They're going to have a baby.

MALCOLM: Shotgun wedding. Nice.

PENNY: He loves her and she loves him.

MALCOLM: That's an excuse for anything, right? Christ. I'm going to the bathroom for a pee. Be a good boy and be gone when I come back.

MALCOLM *exits. Silence.*

LUKE: That was a raging success.

Pause.

TODD: Maybe I should.

PENNY: No. You're staying.

Pause.

TODD: They've done a great job restoring the hotel, haven't they? Was it like this when you were here?

PENNY: Oh, no. It was run down. Not squalid, run down. Sort of nice, like an old friend. All the floorboards squeaked. And the windows would rattle in a strong wind. It was a favourite place then for couples, you know—

LUKE: Dirty weekends?

PENNY: You'd always pick those couples when you served them. Older men, younger women. When they entered the dining room they'd always pause and look around to make sure they didn't know anybody. Then they held hands. Then they relaxed. I felt sorry for their wives. Most of the men were married, the girls single. Duplicity. It was the duplicity I couldn't stand.

TODD: Hey, it's snowing.

PENNY: The tarot reader said it would snow.

LUKE: I didn't know you got a weather forecast when you had a tarot reading.

Jane Harders as Penny and Alex Dimitriades as Todd in the 2004
Griffin Theatre Company production of THE WOMAN WITH DOG'S EYES.
(Photo: Robert McFarlane)

PENNY: It was snowing when we had our wedding night here. It's so long ago and yet… yet I remember standing here and pulling aside the curtain and saying to Malcolm, 'It's snowing'. It was like one of those snowballs, you know, made out of glass. That's the right word, isn't it? Snowballs. It was like it fell especially for me. Luke tell you about Gillian?

TODD: She's not coming.

PENNY: Again. Again. She's more like a ghost than a real daughter-in-law. I like your girl, very much.

TODD: Thanks. Diane.

PENNY: Diane. Yes. It was in the back of my head but couldn't see the light of day.

She laughs at her own turn of phrase. Pause.

LUKE: Mum… either one or the other.

PENNY: I can handle both. It's not the whisky, it's my excitement. All of you here. And I'm back here. Why didn't you bring her?

TODD: She thought she may have been a distraction.

PENNY: That's what I was hoping. Where are you going to get married?

TODD: Haven't decided yet.

PENNY: We'll have a talk about it with her. A decent place. And soon. That's what I was trying to remember. I pressed my face up against the window. It was cold. I looked out. There was snow everywhere and the moon was shining on it. Like my own personal snowball. And it was like I was peering into a snow… snow dome. That's the word. Snow dome. Your father thought I was mad.

LUKE: Why?

PENNY: Oh, in the morning. We were walking across the snow on the lawns and I bent down, grabbed a handful of snow and rubbed it over my face. 'Why did you do that for?' he said. 'Because I want to feel snow on my face.' He just shook his head. [*To* TODD] He will come around. You'll see.

LUKE: Can we have a bet on this?

TODD: Where's Keith?

PENNY: Still in his room, I guess.

TODD: He knows?

LUKE: He knows.

TODD: I feel like a shag on a rock.

LUKE: Well, you'll have to wait.

MALCOLM *enters and goes to top up his whisky.*

MALCOLM: I blink but you're still here. I pinch myself and you're still not gone.

PENNY: You asked me what I wanted for my wedding anniversary. Todd, is it?

MALCOLM: Your wish is my command. Forty years of peace and understanding. [*Pause.*] So, what are you doing for a quid?

TODD: Cleaning.

MALCOLM: Doing it or owning it?

TODD: I clean offices.

MALCOLM: Marvellous where a university education can get you. And what are you doing here?

TODD: Seeing if I exist.

> *Pause.*

MALCOLM: You've become cryptic since you've been a cleaner.

TODD: I don't exist. You made sure I didn't in that magazine piece. Keith exists, Luke exists. Mum exists. But I don't. You talk about Keith and Luke but don't mention me.

MALCOLM: Must have slipped my mind.

TODD: Slipped your mind? Crap. You're like one of those Stalinists who rub out images of their enemies in photographs.

MALCOLM: Stalin now? What next, Hitler?

TODD: All those pictures of the family on the mantelpiece—not one included me.

MALCOLM: You've got good eyes. Ask your mum. She must have been the Stalinist.

> *Pause.*

TODD: It was you?

PENNY: Your father said I had to put them away for the magazine photographer. I was sick to my stomach about it.

TODD: I don't blame you.

MALCOLM: Did you want me to mention you? Did you want me to talk about you stealing my car and crashing it—?

TODD: For Christ sakes—

MALCOLM: How you cheated on your university exams. Stole from my company. Put your brothel visits on the company card.

TODD: It was difficult for me. I lost my way.

MALCOLM: Get a compass. [*To* PENNY] I didn't tell you about the brothels, did I?

PENNY: That was then.

MALCOLM: People don't change.

TODD: Look, all I wanted was to be mentioned as your son.

MALCOLM: Why?

TODD: Because you made me seem as if I didn't exist. That I had never existed.

MALCOLM: That interview had nothing to do with you. That was to present us as a united family. It was just public relations. It had everything to do with a new project of mine. You would have just muddied things.

TODD: Muddied things?

MALCOLM: You've always left behind messes. How many times has Luke had to clean up after you?

TODD: Luke is my younger brother. Do you know how humiliating it is to have to kow-tow to your younger brother. Please, Luke, can I have petrol money for the company car?

MALCOLM: I trust him with money, not you.

TODD: No, you made sure it was Luke, not Keith. You wanted to humiliate me.

MALCOLM: You're fucking lucky. Keith wouldn't have given you a cent—he would have told you to hitchhike.

TODD: And you find that funny?

MALCOLM: I do actually. I'm finding things funnier day by day.

TODD: So people do change?

MALCOLM: Depends on the circumstances.

PENNY: For goodness sake, Malcolm. You're always complaining about Keith and Luke not giving you a grandchild. Todd will. He is.

MALCOLM: What sort of monster would that Boyce be?

PENNY: It would have your genes.

MALCOLM: He's got my genes and look what happened.

PENNY: Oh, you're a cold man. A cold man.

MALCOLM: [*to* TODD] What does your incubator do?

PENNY: What's he on about?

TODD: Diane. Her name's Diane.

MALCOLM: Well?

TODD: She cleans with me.

MALCOLM: You two must have a lot to talk about when you get home.

TODD: We do it part-time.

MALCOLM: Of course, full-time would be—

TODD: Because we're also studying.

MALCOLM: Did they accept you back at uni?

TODD: I'm studying design. So's Diane.

PENNY: He's done some beautiful drawings.

MALCOLM: Of what?

TODD: Interiors. Stuff you don't care about.

MALCOLM: I have poofters to do that for me.

PENNY: You know he has an excellent eye.

MALCOLM: Eye? Last time he took me to an exhibition he said it was the cutting edge of art. There was a guy on a hunger strike who had been in a glass cage for a week and his art was his urine collected in bottles.

LUKE *laughs.*

Cutting edge? Barking mad.

TODD: He was making a statement.

MALCOLM: I can see it as the new fashion in home design. No toilets. Just bottles.

Pause.

TODD: I know about design. You don't. I have a good eye.

MALCOLM: What of your girlie?

PENNY: Her stuff's very nice, too.

MALCOLM: When do you think you'll finish your course?

TODD: Haven't put a time frame on it yet. It's hard going doing the two things.

MALCOLM: What happens when the kid arrives?

TODD: It'll be tight.

MALCOLM: It sure will. You still owe me money.

PENNY: Malcolm!

MALCOLM: A deal's a deal. He made a promise. You were there, Luke.

PENNY: Surely, you can forget it—

MALCOLM: He stole money from me.

> *Pause.*

TODD: [*to* PENNY] He's right. I've started paying it back. It may take a while.

MALCOLM: It's not the thought that counts. It's the deed.

LUKE: Good for you, boy.

TODD: Don't call me boy.

MALCOLM: You wearing that?

TODD: What do you mean?

MALCOLM: This is a special occasion. It's me and your mum's fortieth. Couldn't you have tried, at least for your mum.

TODD: I don't have a tuxedo.

MALCOLM: [*to* LUKE] Can't you rent him one here?

LUKE: This is hippyville. The only tuxedo they'd have would be tie-dyed.

PENNY: As long as he's here.

MALCOLM: You couldn't have said anything more predictable.

> KEITH *enters in tuxedo and coat.*

I'm a cold man, Keith.

LUKE: Fortinbras, you're too late, Hamlet's dead.

> *Pause.*

TODD: Hi, Keith.

KEITH: Todd.

MALCOLM: You were in this, too?

KEITH: Luke and Mum.

MALCOLM: At least you're not betraying me behind my back.

> KEITH *goes to get himself a drink.*

Are you?

LUKE: It wasn't betrayal.

MALCOLM: Then what was it?

KEITH: [*to* TODD] Where's your tux?

PENNY: He can't afford one.

KEITH: So did you just come for the crackers? [*Toasting*] *Salut!*

LUKE: Those French lessons came in handy.

MALCOLM: He came because he thinks he doesn't exist.

PENNY: He came because he wants to be part of the family. And I want him to be part of it, too.

KEITH: You're after a job.

Pause.

TODD: I'm not after anything.

PENNY: Why don't you give him a job? A proper job.

MALCOLM: It would defeat the purpose of him paying me back the money he stole.

PENNY: You want your pound of flesh.

MALCOLM: I want my pounds. [*Pause.*] You're serious?

PENNY: Yes.

Pause.

MALCOLM: It's the wrong time to be talking about it.

PENNY: When will be the right time?

MALCOLM: Not now.

PENNY: When?

MALCOLM: When he finishes his course. Whenever that will be.

PENNY: That's not the way I want it to go.

MALCOLM: You don't fucking what?

PENNY: Don't swear at me.

MALCOLM: Who are you to tell me about my business?

PENNY: This is not business. This is family. [*Pause.*] He's not an employee, he's our son. Don't push him.

KEITH: Why, is he breakable?

LUKE: You attempted it once. Do you want to have another go?

KEITH: What are you talking about, Lukie?

LUKE: You tried to strangle him.

MALCOLM: Is this leading to a joke?

LUKE: A few days before you fired him. I came into Keith's office and he had his hands around Todd's throat. He was purple. I had to pry you off him.

KEITH: A joke.

LUKE: You were deadly serious, Keith.

PENNY: You did that?

KEITH: I was the one! I was the one who found out that he stole that money. Not Dad. Me. I was going to teach him a lesson for letting us down. He always lets us down.

PENNY: You tried to kill him?

KEITH: I kept on asking him over and over, 'Did you steal that money?' He kept lying. I had to belt it out of him.

PENNY: Did you know about this?

MALCOLM: No.

LUKE: I told you.

MALCOLM: You said they were fighting. They were always fighting.

LUKE: I said Keith was trying to strangle him.

KEITH: I lost my temper. I'd had enough of his lying. His cheating.

PENNY: Todd, is this true?

TODD: I was going to pay it back. I told him I would. He started to abuse me. Hit me. And next thing I know is that he's got his hands around my throat. He meant it all right. I could see it in his eyes. He kept saying over and over, 'I'm going to kill you'.

KEITH: It was just a threat.

TODD: Same as when we were young. [*To* PENNY] Remember when you had to pull him off me? He was shoving that dirt down my throat. Same look, same purpose.

KEITH: He stole.

PENNY: For God's sake, he's your brother.

KEITH: I lost my temper, but I had no intention of killing him.

LUKE: Teaching Toddie a lesson.

KEITH: Just shut up. In stealing from the company he was stealing from me, you, Dad.

LUKE: It was a pissy amount.

MALCOLM: It was the final straw, Luke. You know that.

TODD: Those two were earning twenty times what you doled out to me.

MALCOLM: Because they deserved it.

TODD: And I didn't?

MALCOLM: No. You strolled in at all hours. Left whenever you wanted to.

TODD: Because I was treated like dirt. I had to drive Keith or Luke around like a chauffeur. I was just a glorified office boy.

MALCOLM: I said if you came on board you had to start at the bottom.

TODD: They didn't.

MALCOLM: They got uni degrees. They stuck it out. They had the qualifications.

TODD: You didn't.

MALCOLM: Can you believe his cheek? It's my company. I started it. I worked hard. Penny, confirm.

PENNY: No one can ever deny that.

MALCOLM: My father was a train driver, Todd—

TODD: Christ—

MALCOLM: Never took one day off work—

TODD: I know—

MALCOLM: He instilled in me that work is life. It's not playing.

TODD: Give me a chance. Give me a proper job.

MALCOLM: You don't have it.

TODD: Have what?

MALCOLM: The thing inside. That adrenaline buzz when you walked around a work site. I still get it every time I step on a site. I know that if it wasn't for me there would be no work site, there would be no apartments or houses. It never stops, that buzz. That pride. I'm a proud man. I have every right to be proud. There are thousands of people living in my homes, working in my offices. I'm bursting with pride because of that. I'm not ashamed that I like that feeling, no matter what friends say.

TODD: You don't have friends, you have acquaintances.

MALCOLM: You sound like Luke.

LUKE: Is that a compliment?

MALCOLM: [*motioning to the photograph*] That fellow there—he would have felt that buzz, every time he walked around his hotel.

KEITH: Didn't he go broke doing it?

MALCOLM: Not the point. He created this, so that we could be here.

LUKE: Do you get that buzz, Keith? Don't look at me like that.

KEITH: Are you sure Luke's not the product of a quickie with the TV repairer?

PENNY: Your father has been my only lover.

LUKE: What about when you separated that time?

PENNY: I waited for him to call. And he did.

LUKE: Never tempted?

PENNY: Never, Luke. I am a one-man woman and will go to my grave like that.

LUKE: It's admirable.

PENNY: I never know when you're being sarcastic or not.

LUKE: I mean it, I find it admirable. I would like a woman like that.

PENNY: No, you wouldn't.

LUKE: I think I know my own mind.

PENNY: You want a woman to betray you. That will confirm all your worst fears. You actually don't like people, Luke, that's why you get pleasure out of people confirming your worst expectations. I remember when your father promised to take you skating. [*To* MALCOLM] Remember? He sat on the verandah steps waiting for you to come home from work and take him to the rink. He had brand new skates, brand new everything. You sat there for hours until it was time for dinner. You came inside whistling and put the skates into the refrigerator freezer and said, 'That was one of Dad's better promises'. You were in a happy mood for the next week. You see, it proved that your dad's promises were hollow.

MALCOLM: I don't remember that.

PENNY: Because he never mentioned to you but he stored it up in that head of his. Every hurt you get confirms your pessimism about humans.

LUKE: Those therapy sessions of yours have borne strange fruit. And by the way, Keith, I have a bone to pick with you. How come you think I was the product of a TV repairer's loins, why not the pest exterminator? They have all those poisons oozing out of their pores.

MALCOLM: I didn't know I promised.

PENNY: You did.

LUKE: I forgive you, Dad, even though I had the potential to be a world-class skater.

TODD: I didn't know you were interested in skating.

LUKE: Girl skaters have really short skirts.

PENNY: If you married you wouldn't be so flippant.

LUKE: Well, if anything's put me off marriage, it's that comment. You going to marry this chick of yours, Todd? The last thing we want in this family is a bastard.

PENNY: They're going to marry. Then it's your turn.

LUKE: How you two stayed together for forty years is a miracle and I see Keith's marriage and I know marriage is not for me.

KEITH: Keep your comments about my marriage to yourself.

LUKE: How can I? How can I not when your wife breaks down and cries in my office. I liked Gillian's description of you in the magazine article: 'Sensitive. Forthright.' What sort of drugs was she on then?

KEITH: One more word.

MALCOLM: Keith's right. It's enough about her.

> MALCOLM *picks up his bow tie from the table. Even though it is a clip-on he is still finding it difficult.* LUKE *motions to the bottle of whisky for anyone who wants a drink.*

LUKE: Top up?

> KEITH *doesn't.*

Now, don't be sulky.

Toby Schmitz (left) as Luke and Jack Finsterer as Keith in the 2004 Griffin Theatre Company production of THE WOMAN WITH DOG'S EYES. (Photo: Robert McFarlane)

MALCOLM *is okay but* PENNY *holds out her glass.* LUKE *is reluctant to give her more.*

PENNY: It's my party.

LUKE: I thought it was both of yours.

PENNY: It's our party.

LUKE: A splash.

MALCOLM: Penny.

PENNY *looks across and immediately knows what* MALCOLM *wants—help with the bow tie. She helps him.*

You'd think they could invent something simpler.

LUKE: Paint it on, perhaps.

MALCOLM: First time I ever wore a tuxedo—rented, of course—

PENNY: You looked like a movie star.

MALCOLM: —I felt the ant's pants.

PENNY: There. Still do. Distinguished.

LUKE: Sprightly.

MALCOLM: Only men over eighty years old are called sprightly.

He gets his tuxedo jacket from the chair and takes a small, thin package out of it.

LUKE: Well, I feel sprightly. And Mum, you look happy. Are you?

PENNY: I am, Luke.

LUKE: [*to* TODD] And what about our interloper? You haven't got a drink. Sorry. [*He pours him one.*] Quiet as a mouse, Todd.

MALCOLM *hands a package to* PENNY.

PENNY: For me?

MALCOLM: There's no one else in the room having their wedding anniversary.

LUKE: You old softie.

PENNY, *opening the gift, finds a diamond necklace.*

PENNY: Oh, it's beautiful. Beautiful. [*Kissing him*] Oh, thank you. Thank you.

MALCOLM: Years old. Art Deco.

PENNY: Yes, I know. I know. [*Showing it*] Boys.

TODD: Exquisite.

PENNY: It is. It is. Malcolm.

She signals MALCOLM *to put it around her neck, which he does.*

Is my frock good enough for this?

TODD: It's perfection.

MALCOLM: Christ, the lock's too small.

LUKE: I'll do it.

LUKE *takes over and clips up the necklace.*

PENNY: [*to* MALCOLM] You must go to an optometrist.

LUKE: [*re: the necklace*] Did you know how many black South Africans had to die to get these diamonds?

PENNY: Well, it was worth it.

LUKE: There.

She looks in the mirror.

TODD: See, you look grand.

PENNY: I look grandmotherish?

LUKE: Mum, take a compliment.

PENNY: Yes, I know. I must. [*To* MALCOLM] It is very beautiful.

LUKE: What did you give Dad?

PENNY: Todd. [*Pause. Laughing*] That new coat there. It's from Italy. The other one was looking… decrepit.

LUKE: [*feeling it*] Like a warm animal.

Pause.

MALCOLM: You see, if you weren't here this would all be a lot simpler.

Pause.

TODD: [*realising*] You're referring to me?

PENNY: Malcolm, don't.

MALCOLM: It's the truth. I'm not angry, just stating a fact. I've been doing a lot of thinking lately. This new project is going to be very, very tough. And I'll need all the support I can get. If we lose our nerve, then we could lose everything. [*To* LUKE] I want you on the Board of Directors.

Pause.

LUKE: Me?

KEITH: You want him on the Board with me?

MALCOLM: You're not allowed to say no. [*Pause.*] It'll be more responsibility than you've ever had. You don't step back from things.

KEITH: No, he steps aside or around—anything but confront.

MALCOLM: You are a man of strong convictions, Keith. You are constantly saying that we should have nothing to do with this project.

TODD: Is this the one that the newspapers are having a field day with?

KEITH: Yes. And they can ruin us.

MALCOLM: Not if we stand together.

KEITH: You have to listen to what I say.

MALCOLM: I do. But I know you, Keith. You could turn against me.

KEITH: Not against you—against the project.

MALCOLM: I need someone I can turn to in a Board meeting who will support me. Luke will. He doesn't flinch.

KEITH: Because it's just a game to him.

MALCOLM: Well, I like to play.

PENNY: Do you want to do it, Luke?

MALCOLM: Penny!

PENNY: Luke?

LUKE: Sure. No, I want to be on the Board. I don't want Keith to have all the fun.

MALCOLM: Good. Good. You see, this is an important occasion. Fortieth and all that. We will show the enemy just what the Boyces can do.

LUKE: Gee, do you think our fraternal love can survive this, Keith?

KEITH: I will treat you with the respect that you deserve.

LUKE: Supplication is not necessary. You probably get enough of that from your wife.

KEITH: Shut up! Shut up!

PENNY: Keith.

KEITH: None of you know what it's like. You think Gillian's weak, no she isn't. She wants to have control over me. Something good just has to happen with me and she goes mad. It happens time and time again. I have good news and then she reverts and suddenly there's her *I'm going mad baby doll voice*. The talking in her sleep. Not just words, whole monologues, and next morning, there she is, drifting around the house, thinking she's in London or anywhere except where she really is. Won't eat her food, 'cause she thinks I'm poisoning her. I have to beg her to eat anything. But she doesn't because she wants me to use force and when that fails she threatens to kill herself. Always hanging over me is the threat she'll go mad.

And she uses it. And if she's not loony, we go out and she makes an exhibition of herself. She makes it damn clear she's not wearing panties—crossing, uncrossing her legs in front of every guy. Drinks everything in sight. Yells and screams with laughter, thinking she's the queen of the party and always with one eye on me, testing my patience, desperately wanting me to lose my temper so she can point to everyone and go, 'There, that's the real Keith I have to live, my secret tormentor, the one who drives me to the nut house'. And she pushes and pushes, flirting and kissing guys until I want to fucking burst. But I don't. I have learnt that if I lose control, she will win. And this is every single day—that is, if she isn't in some private asylum enjoying the fact that she thinks she's a victim. But you know, her threats of madness are not those of a victim, they are those of a predator fighting to become the one in control. Fighting to cripple me. I have to struggle to maintain a balance with her—but I do. At a cost [*to* PENNY] you don't know, [*to* LUKE] and you have no fucking idea. [*To* MALCOLM] And now you want to control me by having him on the Board.

MALCOLM: He's going on there because of his merits. I don't want to control you.

KEITH: You do, but you won't. I'm too strong for you, just as I'm too strong for Gillian. And as for Luke, I can see his first day on the Board. He'll be wearing pointy-toe shoes, baggy trousers, clown make-up and a red nose.

LUKE: How did he know? He can read my mind.

KEITH: Nothing. Nothing about Gillian or I come at you. I'll come at you so hard.

PENNY: This is a celebration. Your father and I's celebration. So none of that, please.

MALCOLM: And it's a celebration of two sons now being on the Board. [*He pours himself a drink.*] I think a toast is in order.

PENNY: Ying and yang, that's what your father's after, Keith.

LUKE: A Chinese dynasty.

MALCOLM: Your glass is empty, Keith.

> KEITH *reluctantly holds out his glass to be filled when suddenly* LUKE *falls to the floor and thrashes around in an epileptic fit. The family automatically step away leaving him space. They*

have seen this before and wait until the short fit is over. LUKE *lies still on the floor recovering.*

KEITH: Well, that'll go down a treat in the Board room.

A long uncomfortable silence. MALCOLM *pours some drink into* KEITH'*s glass.* LUKE *sits up, a little spaced out, and takes in the grim visages of his family. He smiles.*

LUKE: I was demonstrating a new Mexican dance craze.

He stands up and starts brushing himself down. PENNY *comes over to him and slaps him across the face.*

PENNY: Why did you do that?

LUKE: Why did you do that?

PENNY: You have medication. You don't need to do that! Why aren't you taking your pills? Why do you allow this to happen to you? There's no reason. Why aren't you taking the pills?

Pause.

LUKE: I thought I was over all this.

PENNY: [*kissing him fervently*] Luke. Luke, please don't do this to me. Did you hurt yourself?

LUKE: No, I'm all right.

PENNY: Where are they?

LUKE: In my room.

PENNY: Go take them. Now.

Pause.

LUKE: I didn't want to do this to you on your fortieth. I'm sorry.

MALCOLM: Take your pills, son. Then come back. I want us all to go downstairs to the fireworks together.

PENNY: Here, I'll give you a hand.

LUKE *shakes his head.*

Let me help you.

LUKE: I'm a big boy now.

LUKE *exits. Silence.*

TODD: Has this been happening—?

PENNY: First time in ages. Oh, it's an awful sight. Remember that dreadful time in school...? A teacher came and got you.

TODD: He was all smashed up. The teacher was so scared that she wouldn't touch him. I had to disentangle him from those overturned school desks.

PENNY: And those boys cheering... cheering as he was having the fit. That sort of cruelty would have struck deep into his soul. Deep, so deep. Pitch-black deep. That's what people do—they cheer when you're having a fit. Why does he do this? Why didn't he take them?

TODD: He doesn't like seeming to be at the mercy of anyone or anything.

PENNY: My side of the family, of course.

MALCOLM: Penny. He can control it. It's just that he won't.

KEITH: Do you think you should have put him on the Board?

MALCOLM: He'll take his stuff—

KEITH: I don't care about that. He gets bored easily. He's not diplomatic. Makes all those smart-arse comments all the time.

MALCOLM: He's got a sharp mind.

KEITH: But no mind for details.

MALCOLM: Well, you have. I don't need someone exactly like you on the Board.

KEITH: But why now?

MALCOLM: I said I need every single ounce of support—

KEITH: You don't think I'll support you?

MALCOLM: In these circumstances I have my doubts.

KEITH: Because I can see its flaws.

MALCOLM: Because you can't see its positives. You'll go behind my back to the other Board members.

KEITH: No, I wouldn't.

MALCOLM: You already have.

KEITH: No, I—

MALCOLM: You already have. So don't bullshit me. And you know what? I don't think any less of you. I understand why you're doing it. Luke swings the vote my way.

KEITH: Get out of the deal. The press are crucifying us, so are the environmentalists—

MALCOLM: It's half the fun to beat those dregs.

KEITH: It's not worth it to risk everything. Wait for another opportunity.

MALCOLM: Take too much time. I want it now.

KEITH: Why this urgency?

PENNY: Because he's dying.

Pause.

MALCOLM: What's this? What's this nonsense?

PENNY: You're very sick.

MALCOLM: Do I look sick? [*To* KEITH] Your mother's got rabies, I'm going to have to put her down.

Pause.

PENNY: Luke and I—

MALCOLM: So this is his nonsense?

PENNY: Luke and I were having lunch in the city the other day. Your doctor was in the restaurant and he came over to our table. He seemed very concerned and asked after you. 'How's Malcolm taking things?' I was about to answer when Luke kicked me under the table. He's clever that boy. Luke goes, 'All right, considering his situation,' and your doctor said, 'He's got a big fight on his hands but he's a strong man.' He didn't have to tell us any more. Then he went. Luke said, 'It all makes sense now'. He had heard you crying—

MALCOLM: Crying—when was I fucking crying?

PENNY: He came into your office and heard you smashing up the mirror in your office bathroom and crying. He had never heard you cry before. He said you sounded like an animal that had just been gored. The other night I heard you get out of bed. You went into the living room. I followed you. You were on the couch with your head in your hands.

MALCOLM: And from that you deduce—

PENNY: You're dying. I am hurt, so hurt, Malcolm, that you didn't tell me. I don't want you to go ahead with this project. I want you to come home to me.

MALCOLM: I come home every night. Stop drinking. Jesus…

PENNY: I want to care for you—

MALCOLM: I don't need caring. The reason why I didn't tell you is because it's no concern of yours.

PENNY: I'm your wife.

MALCOLM: It's no concern, because I've got it beat. I have stared it down. I have stared it down so hard that it blinked. It's going. Gone. There would have been a fuss. Now there's no need to fuss. [*To* KEITH] That's why I want that project to go ahead. It's a new beginning. You understand that?

> LUKE *enters.*

> [*To* LUKE] You see, nosy parker, I stared it down and I won.

> LUKE *looks to* PENNY *for an explanation.*

PENNY: I told him we knew.

KEITH: Is that the truth?

MALCOLM: Yes.

PENNY: I don't mind you lying to me, but I loathe you lying to yourself.

MALCOLM: Have another drink.

> *Pause.*

PENNY: I have enough, thank you. I prayed for you. I got down on my hands and knees—like a child—and I prayed for you. Like a little, frightened girl.

MALCOLM: What do you mean?

PENNY: That you wouldn't die.

MALCOLM: It must have worked because I didn't. I won't.

LUKE: Ever?

MALCOLM: Not if I can help it. Because there's nothing after it.

LUKE: No heaven, no hell?

MALCOLM: Hell is merely an adult's version of a kid afraid of monsters under his bed. And the only people who believe in heaven anymore are Muslim terrorists. [*Pause. To* TODD] Don't you have to go and get your coat?

TODD: It's there.

> *Pause.*

PENNY: You don't like his coat?

MALCOLM: Penny, please… [*To* TODD] Why don't you go downstairs and see if everything's ready for the fireworks? We'll meet you down there.

TODD: You mean, send me on an errand.

MALCOLM: Just to make sure everything's ready.

TODD: They'll be fine. I'll walk down with Mum.

Pause.

MALCOLM: Well, you're here, then.

TODD: Yes, your flesh and blood stands before you.

Pause.

MALCOLM: This close shave… it makes things black and white. This is how the spread goes. [*Pointing to* LUKE *and* KEITH] You two will get an equal division of the spoils. Boyce will be the both of you. That's why you're going on the Board.

PENNY: What are these spoils?

MALCOLM: The company. I am making out a will that gives it to these two.

PENNY: And what of Todd?

MALCOLM: I thought the magazine article made it quite clear.

TODD: I don't exist.

MALCOLM: [*to* PENNY] Why did you have to bring him?

PENNY: Because he's your son.

MALCOLM: [*to* TODD] At least you got it straight from me.

KEITH: So it's Luke and me?

MALCOLM: You want more?

KEITH: How will it work—us two?

MALCOLM: I've still got to finesse the details.

PENNY: This is heartless.

MALCOLM: This is the reality of running a business. It's not Todd's forte.

Pause.

TODD: I want to become successful.

MALCOLM: You want money. And you know what I suspect? Your girl got money?

TODD: We're students, I told you.

MALCOLM: She's behind this.

TODD: Diane?

MALCOLM: She knows I'm wealthy. That's why she's not here. She has sent you on an errand. She wants you back in the family so she can marry money. Plenty of women are like that.

TODD: You are totally wrong.

MALCOLM: Am I? Why's she not here, then?

TODD: Because I told her if she came you would try and drive a wedge between us.

MALCOLM: How could I have done that?

TODD: Criticised me in front of her. Charmed her and at the same time damned me. Made me look little, made yourself look big.

MALCOLM: She wants the money, boyo. She wants to become a Boyce.

TODD: You have a mind that is quite...

MALCOLM: Quite, what?

TODD: Cynical.

MALCOLM: No, quite sharp. I read people really well, Todd. And at the bottom, everyone wants something. She wants money.

TODD: You haven't even met her, for goodness sake.

PENNY: You are very wrong, Malcolm.

MALCOLM: I think I will prove to be right. At least Keith married someone who had her own money. [*Tapping his head*] Nous, Todd. Nous.

TODD: You know, when I saw that article and you didn't mention me, I wanted to kill myself.

MALCOLM: Always the easy way out—

TODD: I thought in killing me I'd kill you.

MALCOLM: A strange logic.

TODD: But then I realised you wouldn't care.

PENNY: He would. He would have.

TODD: No, it just would have made it easier for him and those two.

    Pause.

PENNY: I will leave you if you don't treat him properly.

MALCOLM: Don't be silly.

PENNY: Silly, stupid, that's all I am.

MALCOLM: [*to* KEITH] You talk to her.

TODD: And what about you two—what do you think?

KEITH: I think, Todd, that Dad's made the right decision.

TODD: This is what you've always wanted—only I can't see you sharing it.

MALCOLM: They have to. Don't you get it? You don't have the mind for the job—

TODD: No, I'm stupid—

MALCOLM: It's not about intelligence, it's about the cast of mind. You don't know what it's like to get your mind dirty. I'm not talking about scrubbing or real dirt. I mean shaking hands with a greedy politician and not feeling as if you have to immediately rush off to the bathroom and wash the filth off your hands. Or having to deal with a union organiser who is threatening to have his union go on strike over not enough toilet paper when all he wants is a kickback and he's got half a dozen Samoan goons there as reinforcers. You have to have the stomach for that. Keith has one way of dealing with it and Luke another.

TODD: I can offer other things.

MALCOLM: Like what?

TODD: I know the world of design. I know more than Luke or Keith knows about it. I can offer those things, they can't.

MALCOLM: Maybe you can. And maybe you, Todd, have a special ability that would be a good mix with your brothers. Maybe on the Board the responsibility will be the making of you. I don't know why I didn't see that before. What do you think, Todd? [*Pause.*] Can you learn to lie like I just did? Look someone straight in the eye and tell them those most goddam lies? You couldn't look anyone in the eye.

   Pause. TODD *laughs.*

TODD: Can you do that, Luke?

LUKE: Keith and I both can. But for different reasons. Keith regards it as a war. It amuses me.

TODD: I thought you'd say that.

LUKE: It's a game based on money. People think this era is obsessed with sex. It's obsessed with money. It always has been and always will be. Men and women equally. It's just a question of how much they'll sell their souls for. You know that joke. Ask a woman if she'd sleep with a strange man for three hundred dollars. What do you think I am—a prostitute, she says. What about a million dollars? Well maybe, she says. You say: now that we know what you are, all we're doing now is haggling over the price.

TODD: I don't believe what you've said. I don't believe you even believe it.

LUKE: You don't know me, Todd, because deep down I do believe it.

TODD: Not everyone is like that.

LUKE: That's why you couldn't cut it.

PENNY: Are you saying that your father's right in what he's doing?

LUKE: I'm saying that Todd wears his heart on his sleeve. This business is tough going. Especially now. It's the biggest gamble we've ever taken. Look at Keith. He's is not a coward but he's backing away from this battle.

KEITH: I'm trying to make sure we don't lose everything.

PENNY: I don't care. These three boys are your sons, Malcolm. All three. Todd will make good. He is different—they're all different, but all three are our flesh and blood. You have to listen to me: I brought the boys up by myself. You were never home.

MALCOLM: I worked hard for us. Look what I've got us. We have one of the best houses in Sydney—

PENNY: I understood that you worked hard. You don't think that I realise that every time I look back at our beginning when we had nothing. Now we've got anything we can possibly ask for and I'm grateful, so grateful for what we've got. I admire you absolutely for that. I think you're a great man, Malcolm, but we must keep our family together. What if you were about to die—those two don't have any children—

MALCOLM: They will.

PENNY: Oh, I know different. Luke won't. Will you, Luke? He doesn't like himself enough to have children. Keith will—eventually, but Todd is having a child. A grandchild. And that child carries your name.

MALCOLM: It's so simplistic, what you're saying, it's so kindergarten.

PENNY: You are the kind of man who cannot admit, even to yourself, what you truly think.

MALCOLM: I speak my mind. Everyone knows that.

PENNY: I mean… what you really think deep in your heart.

MALCOLM: [to LUKE] You took your mother's side in this. You could have refused to bring him up here.

PENNY: He did the right thing.

MALCOLM: Right thing! Right thing! This was supposed to be perfect. A perfect evening. Everything's arranged. The fireworks, the orchestra… And you mess it all up. As you do.

PENNY: I am fighting here. I am fighting for our son.

MALCOLM: A losing battle. What's got into you? Why are you like this suddenly?

PENNY: I don't know… I don't know, Malcolm.

Pause.

TODD: You shouldn't have done that interview. You shouldn't have made me vanish like that.

MALCOLM: On and on about it.

TODD: It was the final straw. Ever since we were young you've been working at making me vanish until you completed the job with that interview.

MALCOLM: Making you vanish—

TODD: I thought nothing could have been worse than what you did to me that day you had lunch with the Premier—

MALCOLM: You didn't miss much.

TODD: I missed everything. I drove you and Luke and Keith to the restaurant and you told me to wait in the car. Like some chauffeur. Three hours and you come outside, you three, pissed and happy and you say to me, 'Home, James'.

KEITH: He was being funny.

TODD: Me outside in the car waiting three hours—not a son, a servant. No, he meant it, Keith.

MALCOLM: You wanted to start at the bottom. Anyway, if I'm such a bastard, why do you want to come back? Why do you want to become a Boyce?

TODD: Because I'm having a child. It's changed everything. I want it to know his uncles, his grandmother, his grandfather. I want it to be a Boyce. I want it to be pleased to be a Boyce.

MALCOLM: Very sensitive New Age.

PENNY: Malcolm.

MALCOLM: I'm supposed to fall for that fatherhood gibberish? A changed man because he's got his girl up the duff?

Pause.

TODD: I'll take you to court.

MALCOLM: What in the hell…

TODD: When you're dead.

MALCOLM: What are you going to do—kill me? You wouldn't have the nerve.

TODD: The will. I'll contest the will.

MALCOLM: From the moment you set out here today you've only been after money.

TODD: I'm after being a part of the family.

MALCOLM: Get a load of this guy. On what grounds would you contest my will?

TODD: Cruelty.

MALCOLM: Cruelty? Did I ever hit any of you boys? Well, did I?

TODD: Mental cruelty.

MALCOLM: What did I do? Pull the wings off your favourite butterfly?

TODD: For a start, you always belittled me.

MALCOLM: There was a lot to belittle.

TODD: That's an example. You forced me to play football. You'd drive me to a game and if I was lousy—which was most of the time—I had to walk home. No matter how far away. I was scared of the dark. 'Oh, you're a cry baby.' You locked me in the wardrobe. Do you know how terrified I was? It was like being buried alive. I was so scared that I pissed myself. I sat there for hours, in the dark, in my wet pants. What about when you fired me? You got security guards to throw me off the premises. I go home to see Mum and my paintings that were in the hallway were gone. You burnt them. Another piece of me gone. You know nothing about art. But I'm good at it, but you call me an idiot because of what I like in art. These two are the golden boys. Me, I'm always wrong. It's taken me a long time to try and get my life together. I know sometimes I've been a fool. Stealing that money… I mean, I just did it to annoy you.

MALCOLM: Ten out of ten.

TODD: And sarcasm like that. Your final belittlement was to cut me out of the will.

Pause.

MALCOLM: You'd go to court on that flimsy logic?

TODD: There are countless examples—

MALCOLM: And who'd back you up?

PENNY: I would.

Pause.

MALCOLM: What has got into you?

PENNY: You're acting like a God. Parcelling out favours here, destroying a life there.

MALCOLM: I have every right—

PENNY: With me. Don't forget me. We're husband and wife.

MALCOLM: But why would you speak against me? I mean, what could you say?

PENNY: I will back Todd up. I'd speak about you. About our marriage.

MALCOLM: Marriage? What's that got to do with it?

PENNY: The way you were cruel towards Todd, the way you were cruel towards me.

MALCOLM: Come on, Penny—

PENNY: You deserted me.

MALCOLM: It's our fortieth—

PENNY: Emotionally deserted me.

MALCOLM: I'm here!

PENNY: You may not have hit them, but you hit me. They can vouch for me.

MALCOLM: I was under pressure—

PENNY: You hit me in front of them. Luke? Keith?

MALCOLM: Goaded. You goaded me. Pushed and pushed.

PENNY: I wanted you to talk to me, for God's sake. Just talk. Do you know the sheer loneliness I went through? The hard looks you gave me. Like a basilisk—

MALCOLM: What in the bejesus is that?

PENNY: A reptile, whose stare and breath can kill you.

MALCOLM: You'd go to court with that. I hated it that you gave up so easily. I'd just have to raise my voice and there'd be tears.

PENNY: I didn't know what to do, how to keep you. I shut up about your women.

MALCOLM: What women?

PENNY: Oh, come on. See, right there I can see you're lying. You know why, you stare right at me. I'd ask you if you were seeing a woman and there'd be this stare—you'd look me straight in the eye—as if daring me, as if saying, how stupid can you be, woman. Then the whole temperature of the house would change when you had a woman. You'd be happy, charming, we'd go out, do things together. I didn't know if it was guilt or an overflow of happiness from the other woman which made you do that... who knows? You probably don't know yourself. I didn't know whether to curse your women or thank them. Then they'd be those times, those hard-stare times and I couldn't break down the door to you. I know I goaded, I know I pushed, but I loved you. Then you batter me in turn, calling me stupid, an idiot, just like you did Todd. No wonder I cracked up. No wonder I'm on medication. You're strong, I'm not. I wilted. But you don't know hell until you wake up one sunny morning and all you see is darkness. It's like this black soot seeping into your brain. And you fall, Malcolm. You just freefall into this bottomless pit and then there's this relief because you end up not feeling depressed but feeling nothing at all. And then comes the shock treatment and you start to feel again—there's a brief spark of life—and then blackness, the soot again. You sent me into that darkness. That's why I will not desert Keith's wife, even when he does and he will because I know that Keith is like you—if he senses any weakness in someone he has to crush them. You both have that coldness, that Arctic coldness. That's why you're so good at what you do. Living with you, nothing was certain—what mood is he in, does he have another lover...? You laugh at me and my astrology and tarot, but it gave me certainty. You never gave me that. I had to depend on signs and omens, because I couldn't depend on you. Oh, sometimes, Malcolm, I felt like a prisoner and I wanted release so badly. I wanted to fall, fall from the top of the highest building. Sometimes I'd leave our bed and climb up into the attic and onto the roof and want to jump. But, it wasn't high enough. What if I broke only a few bones, you'd hate me even more for not succeeding. There were times when I'd find myself despising you so much. I hated myself for feeling that because I knew the reason I stayed was because I loved you. When I saw you with your head in your hands that night—in total despair—I had this overwhelming feeling of love and pity for you. For the first time in my life I felt pity for you. And I knew, I know, you are dying. Don't even try to deny it. But you're not going to act like God, lifting up this son, crushing this one. You don't understand, but I do, that this is the important thing, not some empire you're going to force them to build. I want you to set things right. Because if you don't, I will speak about us in court. I will have my moment. It would nearly destroy me to do it but, you know, a part of me would be relieved to speak it. To let everyone know what it was really like. And you know the worst thing? It will be all over the newspapers and on television—the Boyce name will be besmirched and ridiculed. Boyce will become a laughing stock. It would be everything you hate. Everything you fear. I will haunt you after your death.

Silence.

This room. It's right to be back in it. I have this strong, bright memory of you. It's so real I can almost taste it. It's the morning after our wedding night. You are sleeping in the bed. I couldn't sleep because I was so happy. I smelt of you, you were all through me. So strong, so male. I got up and knew, I knew from the moment my feet touched the carpet—it was like my whole body was filled with light—that I was pregnant. And I was right. I looked out the window and it was covered in snow. The sun was out and the snow was almost blinding and there—like something out of a fairytale—was a deer walking through the snow. A real deer. I was so full of love for you, my heart was bursting. [*Pause.*] You cast Todd out, you cast me out. You come home to me for the rest of the time you have. You come home to all of us, including Todd. The three of them are our future. [*Pause.*] There is one other thing, Malcolm, there comes a time when children judge their parents and you don't want to be found wanting by them.

Pause.

MALCOLM: Well, they judge me, then.

Silence.

KEITH: It's time for the firecrackers.

KEITH, LUKE *and* TODD *grab their overcoats.*

PENNY: I love you. I couldn't have said that if I didn't so love you.

He nods.

I know these fireworks, the dinner, the orchestra is all your doing. And I thank you. Accept my thanks.

Pause.

MALCOLM: I do.

TODD: How long do you have?

MALCOLM: Who knows?

TODD: They must have told you.

MALCOLM: Six months. A year. So, you understand, Todd, that everyone has to pull their weight. I don't have enough time on my side to quibble and prevaricate. I only have to do.

LUKE *has grabbed* PENNY*'s overcoat and puts it on her as* MALCOLM *picks up his and starts to button it up.*

PENNY: Thank you, darling.

LUKE: [*looking out the window*] The moon's really big. The firecrackers should look great.

PENNY: It's still snowing?

LUKE: It's what you wanted—isn't it?

KEITH: We'd better hurry downstairs.

They all have buttoned up their coats, MALCOLM *is last. The boys are in various stages of leaving the room, when* MALCOLM *pauses as if deciding on something important.*

MALCOLM: [*to his sons*] Wait. Wait a moment, boys. Penny.

He then starts singing 'Some Enchanted Evening' at first softly. LUKE *laughs as if this is meant to be funny but realises that his father means it.* MALCOLM *reaches full voice—even though it is not beautifully sung, he means it.*

> Some enchanted evening
> You may see a stranger,
> You may see a stranger
> Across a crowded room.
> And somehow you know,
> You know even then
> That somewhere you'll see her again and again.

> Some enchanted evening
> Someone may be laughing,
> You may hear her laughing,
> Across a crowded room.

And night after night,
As strange as it seems
The sound of her laughter will sing in your dreams.

PENNY *and her sons react in their own way. The lights begin to change to the exterior as he sings. The five stand in the snow as snow flakes fall on them. They look up at the moonlit sky as the fireworks explode. All fades into darkness.*

THE END

THE MARVELLOUS BOY

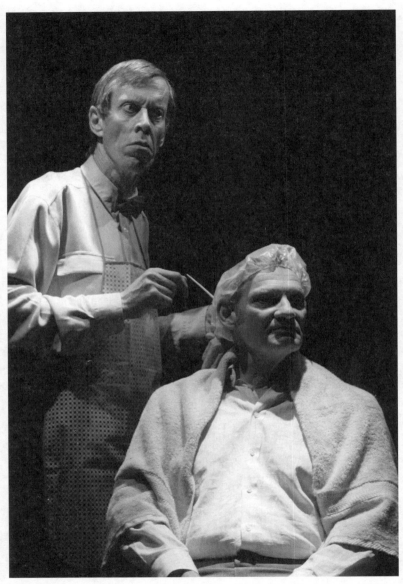

Bruce Spence (left) as Ray and Anthony Phelan as Victor in the 2005 Griffin Theatre Company production of THE MARVELLOUS BOY. (Photo: Robert McFarlane)

FIRST PRODUCTION

The Marvellous Boy was first produced by Griffin Theatre Company at the SBW Stables, Sydney, on 13 October 2005 with the following cast:

LUKE	Toby Schmitz
MALCOLM	Danny Adcock
RAY	Anthony Phelan
VICTOR / BAIN CIPOLLA	Bruce Spence
ESTHER	Susie Lindeman

Director, David Berthold
Designer, Nicholas Dare
Lighting Designer, Matthew Marshall

CHARACTERS

MALCOLM BOYCE, 60s
LUKE BOYCE, youngest son, early 30s
RAY POLLARD, mid-40s
BAIN CIPOLLA, middle-aged
VICTOR, 40s
ESTHER TUCKER, 40s

SETTING

Time: now.

SCENE ONE

The top of Sydney Tower. Day. MALCOLM BOYCE *enters with his son* LUKE.

LUKE: Why did you want to meet up here?

MALCOLM: I like the view. You can see all of Sydney from here. See, right out to the Blue Mountains. The Northern beaches. Over the city, suburbs. [*Pointing*] Built that. Built that. And there, see, with the naked eye, Hesperus Park.

LUKE: The eye of the storm.

MALCOLM: The eye of the storm.

Pause.

LUKE: I don't think I've ever been up here before.

MALCOLM: Yes you have, son. When you were a kid. You went on some sort of school excursion.

LUKE: Don't remember.

MALCOLM: Your teacher fainted.

LUKE: That's right. I kept on throwing myself against the windows to see if I'd bounce off. The more she screamed, the more I did it.

MALCOLM: I had to deal with the headmaster. I said you didn't mean to make her faint, it was just that you were fearless.

LUKE: I opt for the theories of stupidity and the fact that I hated that teacher. It's all coming back. She fainted over there. It meant we all got to look up her dress. She had white panties on with the words 'Plumbers' Entrance' sown into them in bright red letters. Apostrophe after the s, which meant she had expected more than one plumber.

MALCOLM: Really?

LUKE: Surely my unformed mind couldn't have invented such explicit detail.

MALCOLM: No, you were fearless. Throwing yourself against the windows like that. It's what I like about you, Luke. Which is why we're here. I need you to do that for me. This fellow who's coming here... his name's Ray Pollard. A bit of a hard nut. I need you to liaise with him for me.

LUKE: Doing what?

MALCOLM: We can't go back now.

LUKE: Back from where?

MALCOLM: [*pointing*] There. Hesperus Park. Your brothers don't know this... the banks won't lend me any more money. We're losing thousands of dollars per day because we can't build there. Those environmentalists are driving me fucking crazy. And the thing that's truly getting to me—besides the fact they could drive us bankrupt— is the information they have. Where are they fucking getting such inside information about me... about the company...? Every time I see that spokesman—Cipole, Cippola, whatever he's fucking called—on TV, I want to strangle him. I mean, what gives him the damn right to do this to us? What fucking right does he have to take the high moral ground? We have done everything to make sure what we're doing is environmentally friendly... Friendly? We're bending over backwards like some fucking pillow-biter. The newspapers are taking their side—they love all this inside information stuff... making us seem like some family from hell...

LUKE: We just have to match their PR. Ride it out.

MALCOLM: Luke, I don't have the time and, more importantly, our company doesn't. Now, this Ray fellow is necessary. He will do the things that have to be done. He's fearless too. Unlike your brothers you won't close your eyes.

LUKE: What do you mean?

> RAY POLLARD *enters.*

RAY: Holy Jesus, this is fucking high.

MALCOLM: Ray...

RAY: Oh, Jesus, Jesus... Why are we meeting here, Malcolm? Whoa, how can you stand to be up so high? Vertigo is a weakness, I freely admit to such sensations. I'm going nowhere near those windows.

MALCOLM: Ray, this is my son Luke.

LUKE: Hello, Ray.

RAY: Luke.

MALCOLM: The reason we're up here, Ray, is that I want to point out something.

RAY: Well, get it over and done with. I'm not staying up in this aerie a moment longer than the dictates of necessity. [*To* LUKE] By the way, congratulations.

LUKE: For what?

RAY: Aren't you getting married soon? I was perusing the papers—

MALCOLM: That's Todd, my middle son.

RAY: [*to* LUKE] Just as well—don't. Gee, I wonder how they clean the windows up this high. I hear this tower moves in the wind. [*Noticing a woman, offstage*] She's got nice big mammaries... must be still breast feeding.

MALCOLM: Ray...

RAY: All ears.

MALCOLM: [*pointing*] See that distant park there... behind that thin, grey building?

RAY: That's Hesperus Park.

MALCOLM: You know?

RAY: Can't fail to, Malcolm. There's stuff about it in the papers every day. Your *bête noire*.

MALCOLM: I've done everything right. Played by the rules. I need you to help me on this one. I don't have all the energy I want. The chemo therapy is exhausting.

RAY: Yes, I've heard it's enervating.

MALCOLM: I want you to liaise with Luke, instead of me. I want you to take him under your wing. Teach him the ropes. Teach him what has to be done in circumstances like this. You understand?

RAY: Loud and clear. You don't think this thing is moving, do you? Have they done structural tests on this thing? You'd know about that.

MALCOLM: I don't know. So is it a deal?

RAY: Love to.

MALCOLM: There's a fellow called Cipolla—

RAY: Yes, I've heard some of his scurrilous remarks about you. Don't worry, after the head goes, the body shrivels. Luke'll look after the financial aspects?

MALCOLM: Of course.

RAY: Well, Luke, we look like becoming buddies, to use a common parlance. Why don't you send him around tonight, Malcolm. I'll induct him into my world. Must go. This tower is unsafe. I can feel it. We are embarking on a wonderful relationship, my marvellous boy. I'll be your little ray of sunshine. *Auf Wiedersehen*.

    RAY *exits. Silence.*

LUKE: You have to be kidding.

MALCOLM: He's a bit unconventional.

LUKE: He's insane.

MALCOLM: It's an act. To put people off-guard.

LUKE: Well, it worked on me.

MALCOLM: He has never let me down.

◆ ◆ ◆ ◆ ◆

SCENE TWO

Ray's office above his nightclub. Night. A knock at the door.

RAY: Enter. *Entrez. Avanti!*

> LUKE *enters. Music is heard as the door opens.*

Close the door. Close the door! Can't stand the music.

> LUKE *closes the door and looks around.*

What are you doing here?

LUKE: You asked me to come.

RAY: That's beside the point, whether I asked you to come or not. Or whether it's my place or yours. Whenever you meet someone— shock and awe—just say, 'What are you doing here?' It unsettles anybody. Lesson one.

LUKE: Lesson one?

RAY: Your dad told me to teach you everything I know.

LUKE: So it won't be a long lesson?

> *Pause.*

RAY: I detect superciliousness.

LUKE: Guilty, your honour.

RAY: And never plead guilty.

LUKE: Lesson two?

RAY: Superciliousness mixed with contempt. A potent cocktail. A libation?

LUKE: A drink, yes. No water, no ice.

RAY: A man after my own heart.

> *He pours drinks.*

LUKE: What exactly do you do, Ray?

RAY: You heard of the term pyromaniac?

LUKE: You like to light fires?

RAY: I'm a pyromaniac of the mind. Though, you will notice, if you are ever to see my naked torso, one fire was almost the death of me.

LUKE: I like scars.

RAY: I will titillate you with promises of seeing my scar tissue over the course of your apprenticeship. Suffice... [*Re: the drink*] Enough?

LUKE: Plenty.

RAY: I was starting out. Some guy paid me a hundred dollars to set fire to his nightclub. It was going broke. I was splashing petrol around the stage and then the kitchen and paid little attention to the fumes. I threw a match thinking I would easily outrun the flames. There was this almighty explosion, my clothes burst into flames—always buy wool, never synthetic shirts—

LUKE: I'll remember that—

RAY: And I started to burn. You know what happened?

LUKE: You managed to make your way outside—

RAY: Straight into the hands of a cop. And I said to him—that I was a bystander who rushed in when I heard someone calling out for help. I was mentioned on the news—called a hero. The thing was, they did find a charred body in there.

LUKE: The manager's?

RAY: Never found out.

LUKE: Is there a lesson in that story?

RAY: Well, no. I'm just telling you about my dreadful burns. But by 'do', do you mean, what doth Ray do? After several fires I became a debt collector. I never used force. 'There are other ways to collect payments,' I'd say. And it is interesting to note that none of them asked me about those other ways. Then I managed nightclubs. Now I'm a nightclub owner hence my office here. Keep my finger on the pulse of what is happening downstairs. And what did you notice?

LUKE: Girls waiting around for guys to turn up.

RAY: For mutual hilarity. And, I'm what you might call a 'fixer'.

LUKE: What do you fix? Broken hearts?

RAY: Have done that in my time. Problems, that's what I fix up. Your father's problems, for example.

LUKE: You've been doing it for some time?

RAY: Oh, yes. I had some money tied up in the scaffolding business. You'd know about that?

LUKE: They're always trying to stand over us.

RAY: Not always. Not for a couple of years.

LUKE: You?

RAY: I had a word with a few of those Pacific Islanders. Big laddies, aren't they?

LUKE: That's all you did? Have a word?

RAY: A whisper into their ears.

LUKE: Lesson three—what was the whisper?

RAY: Expired visas.

LUKE: So you don't involve yourself in the rough and tumble, Ray?

RAY: It's for young blokes. I have rarely been tempted to use a handgun.

LUKE: Have you, though?

RAY: Last time was a bloke who double-crossed me. He did it to me several times. I caught him in an alley one night. He was so scared he automatically went into colonic irrigation mode. I said that I promised on my heart that I wouldn't hurt him. He then ran off and I shot him in the leg. 'But you crossed your heart and promised, Ray.' I said, 'What do you mean? I've got no heart.'

LUKE: The moral of the story?

RAY: There are no morals.

Pause.

LUKE: For years with Dad, eh?

RAY: We go back some time. This latest flap is unfortunately a dire situation for your father. But I am on the way to solving it.

LUKE: The last thing we want, Ray, is for you to burn yourself again.

RAY: I do love the aroma of petrol and the perfume of the phosphorous tips of matches. The word you're looking for is 'rococo'. Ornate will do. You expected a drunken, foul-mouthed thug, instead you are being entertained by a charming, feckless man drunk with words. Do you like words, Luke?

LUKE: My lack of ability as a mime artist makes me dependent on them.

RAY: Me too. Similarities are good to find. See that... that dictionary. That has been with me since I was fourteen. Stolen.

LUKE: I wouldn't expect anything less, Ray.

RAY: My mother—the devil preserve her mummified heart—had me out of wedlock and sent me to a Catholic orphanage. I will have nothing bad said about priests. But one had a fixation on my petite buttocks. I had to constantly fight him off. One night in his study I punched him as I fought him off. He hit his head on the desk. Unconsciousness embraced him. I tied him up with the curtain sash, doused him with kerosene from the heater—

LUKE: I'm detecting a pattern here—

RAY: —and lit a candle. Before fleeing, I stole that book because, despite his randy unnatural desires, he told me that if you control language, you control the world. And he's right.

LUKE: You must be King of the World by now.

RAY: Prince, maybe. Duke, certainly. Two things you need in life, my heir apparent, a gun in one hand, a dictionary in the other. One is to kill and the other is to terminate your opponent with verbal acuity.

LUKE: I thought you didn't need a gun?

RAY: I can hold in my head two mutually exclusive notions and synthesize them. Don't think that.

LUKE: Think what?

RAY: That what you are ruminating upon.

LUKE: And what's that?

RAY: Is he for real? [*Pause.*] I am? I am real or faux real? [*Pause.*] I smell something.

LUKE: Petrol?

RAY: Fear. Do you smell it?

LUKE: You think I'm afraid?

RAY: Smell the air, Luke. It's getting stronger. Stench of fear. You have smelt the semen- and vaginal-juice-stained sheets of a hot night? Fear is as rancid and as identifiable an odour as that.

A knock at the door.

Come in!

The door opens.

Close the door!

BAIN, *a scared man, enters.*

What are you doing here?

BAIN: Those men... they pushed me in here.

RAY: You didn't answer my question. [*To* LUKE] My boy, do you smell it now? [*To* BAIN] Pray, sir, what is your name?

BAIN: Bain Cipolla.

RAY: I bet you were teased at school. Kids saying, 'You're the bane of my life', and similar such jocular expressions? True?

BAIN: Yes.

RAY: And you are still a bane, a baneful man? How did you get here?

BAIN: Who are you?

RAY: How did you end up in my neck of the woods?

BAIN: A couple of thugs grabbed me off the street early this morning as I was going to work. They put a gun to my head and shoved me in the boot of their car.

RAY: Why?

BAIN: Why?

RAY: These damn echoes.

LUKE: You used a gun?

RAY: I didn't.

BAIN: I could have suffocated in there. I banged and banged—

RAY: You should have saved your breath. The driver's deaf.

BAIN: What the fuck is going on?!

RAY: Language. Language. Were you afraid?

BAIN: I had my moments.

RAY: So you were. The thing is, Bain, you could have suffocated. Right now you'd be nothing but a malodorous corpse in the boot.

BAIN: What is this about?

RAY: Do you understand what I'm saying—you came very close to carking it. Your job is as the head of a union. True?

BAIN: Yes.

RAY: What you say is law in your union.

BAIN: No. It's a democracy.

RAY: Please, there's grown-ups here. I see you on television and in the newspapers daily. Quite the cock of the walk, you look.

BAIN: Is this about Hesperus Park?

RAY: The old lady at the back of the community hall raises her hand and shouts, 'Bingo!'

BAIN: That development will destroy the park. It's an environmental disaster.

LUKE: Actually, it isn't. The development will keep half of the grasslands and most of the animals. So, I'm right and you're wrong.

BAIN: And who are you?

LUKE: Kang. And this is Kodos. We're aliens. We've come to earth and we're going to give you an anal probe.

BAIN: [*about to go*] I don't have to stay here.

RAY: Those men who escorted you are outside the door. And if you leave before I say, Bain, you could find yourself in a terribly desperate situation. At the moment I'm toying with you. Please don't make my blood boil and curdle.

BAIN: Has that cunt Boyce organised this?

RAY: Where do you get the right to call him that?

BAIN: So he did.

LUKE: I think he's ready for his anal probe.

RAY: Actually it was all my idea. I can't stand your ugly visage. This is the deal, Bain. Your union will stop boycotting the project.

BAIN: The union won't agree—

RAY: Yes, it will. Because if it doesn't, remember this: every single day you'll be looking over your shoulder wondering, waiting, because when I say you'll regret not doing as I say, then your life will be filled with a dread so dark, so insidious, that you'll be rendered impotent in deed and thought. You will be paralysed by an all-consuming fright. I promise you that. My name is Ray, Bain. Remember that. So, we can expect you to make one more statement about the development and that is that you're lifting the boycott. [*Pause.*] Bain.

BAIN: This is unfair.

RAY: Your union is being unfair. So…?

Pause.

BAIN: All right.

RAY: I do suggest that you take a holiday after your statement. It'll do wonders for your sanity.

Pause.

BAIN: Can I go now?

RAY: Yes.

LUKE: No.

RAY: No?

LUKE: Bain, what's been interesting about your attack on the Boyce development is how personal it is. Where do you get all that information?

BAIN: What information?

LUKE: About disagreements in the family over the development. One brother, Keith, opposes it, one brother agrees with it, and how Boyce himself wanted to disinherit the middle son, Todd.

BAIN: I recognise you...

LUKE: And all the dirt about the mother... her times in the sanatoriums.

BAIN: You're the youngest one... Luke. Luke Boyce.

LUKE: Kang, I told you. Did you have a detective?

Pause.

RAY: Answer him or you are back in that car boot. Do you want me to give you a countdown? Three, two...

BAIN: Esther. Esther Tucker.

RAY: Ring a bell?

LUKE: No. Who is she?

BAIN: She's very concerned about this development. She's more than concerned. She's obsessed by it. She seems to know all this personal stuff about your family.

LUKE: You're the frontman.

BAIN: I'm no frontman. I believe in my ideals.

RAY: No Australian has ideals, we're too pragmatic for that. And you're going to be pragmatic.

LUKE: How did she come to be doing this?

BAIN: After the builders' labourers union agreed to give up their boycott, she came to me with all the information and I thought she had a case.

RAY: Well, she's alone now. Isn't she? Yes?

BAIN: Yes.

RAY: Thank you, Bain. The exit is there. Be on your way, my good man, and remember, your lips are sealed about this frank exchange of viewpoints.

BAIN: If I agree, then you won't do anything else to me?

RAY: Drop the boycott and we'll never have to meet again.

BAIN: Thank you.

RAY: You're free to go.

BAIN: Thank you.

> BAIN *exits.*

RAY: Kodos?

> *He laughs, so does* LUKE.

LUKE: First thing I could come up with. Will he—?

RAY: Oh, yes. You can always tell that they'll abide by your command at the end of a meeting—it's the degree of their gratitude. Notice how grateful he was. Anyway, Victor will escort him home as a gentle reminder. Shall we toast our victory?

> *He grabs two glasses and a bottle of whisky.*

I must say how impressed I was by your performance—

LUKE: You seem to know a lot, Ray.

RAY: What I know can be tattooed on one side of my penis.

LUKE: It's that big?

> RAY *gives a glass of whisky to* LUKE.

That's how you've helped my father over the years.

RAY: A decade or so.

LUKE: I underestimated you, Ray.

RAY: My boy, that is always to my advantage.

> *They clink glasses.*

To your development.

◆ ◆ ◆ ◆ ◆

SCENE THREE

Esther's living room. Day. Attractive and intelligent, ESTHER *walks in followed by* MALCOLM, *who takes in the surroundings.*

MALCOLM: Looks different.

ESTHER: Just a coat of paint.

MALCOLM: No, I mean, new furniture. Haven't seen that couch before.

ESTHER: Comfy, isn't it?

MALCOLM: And your hair. You look very well.

ESTHER: Healthy?

MALCOLM: Healthy and… you know, attractive.

ESTHER: That's what women do—when they have to transform their lives, they transform themselves and their surroundings. [*Pause.*] You're full of compliments today. Not like the last time I saw you.

Pause.

MALCOLM: I haven't come to fight.

ESTHER: I should hope not.

MALCOLM: It's just that you seem... I would like to talk without us aggravating each other.

ESTHER: Am I aggravating you?

MALCOLM: Not yet. [*Pause.*] That trade unionist fellow... who was stopping my project... Cipolla... he made an announcement that as far as he was concerned there was no need to stop my development of Hesperus Park.

ESTHER: Bain called me... he sounded very scared and feared for his life. You have something to do with that?

MALCOLM: Why would I? All the other unions have agreed to stop their pickets.

ESTHER: Because you paid them out—

MALCOLM: He knew no one else was going to support him. He'd have to give in eventually.

ESTHER: He told me the day before he rang me that he'd be with me come hell and high water. Hell must have come, eh? When I saw it in the shop I thought it was too red—

MALCOLM: What?

ESTHER: But it brightens up the room. I have decided on bright colours. Why don't you go?

MALCOLM: I will. I will. Believe me, I don't want to stay here longer than is necessary.

ESTHER: Cruelty becomes you. What was Bain threatened with—cutting off his toes? Fingers? Why not bring back medieval punishments—pluck out his eyes?

MALCOLM: Why must you push everything so far?

ESTHER: I want to see where the logic of your behaviour will end. You've looked better.

Pause.

MALCOLM: So this fellow, Chips—

ESTHER: Bain Cipolla—

MALCOLM: —announces that his union is withdrawing its blockade.

ESTHER: Yes, I read the newspapers too.

MALCOLM: And then now it's you. Everywhere I turn, I see your face... your comments about my project, about me... then I realised. You know, I kept on wondering how personal stuff about me, my family, got into the papers—like we were grotesques... Then once you stepped to the fore after Cipolla got his union to back off, it all came to me. You were feeding him that information for months.

ESTHER: Aren't I allowed to present a case against your megalomaniac project?

MALCOLM: You make me out a monster—

ESTHER: I present the facts.

MALCOLM: No, no, don't bullshit me, Esther, this is personal. It's so brilliant the way you've decided to get at me. Lonely, crusading woman devoting all her time to fight the evil empire. They lap it up. The public gets drunk on it.

ESTHER: Did you want a drink?

MALCOLM: You know for a fact that we have commissioned several environmental reports and we're making sure this housing project won't interfere with the life of even one fucking endangered member of the tadpole family or whatever it is.

ESTHER: Now look who's pushing things to extremes. What do you want to do? Found an empire? [*Pause.*] My God, that's what you want to do.

MALCOLM: What's wrong with me wanting to pass my name on?

ESTHER: I knew you had an ego, but I didn't know it was that gigantic. Don't you doubt the idea of it? Don't you have any self-doubt?

MALCOLM: What would that achieve? This project is the culmination of my life's work.

ESTHER: That makes it right?

MALCOLM: Yes. Yes, because I have abided by the rules, you're not.

ESTHER: Rules? You probably paid off those environmental scientists.

MALCOLM: Wrong—

ESTHER: All of that park should be saved. What about during the building of the houses—it's going to destroy the ecosystem around it.

MALCOLM: When did you become so interested in this environment thing? You never talked about it to me. Not once. This is my monument—

ESTHER: Boyce Park.

MALCOLM: That's when I knew it was you giving all that personal stuff to the papers. Only my family and you knew that I was changing the name of the park.

ESTHER: The second-last time we were together. Puffed-up pride—I'm calling it Boyce, you bragged.

MALCOLM: My boys are going to carry my name.

ESTHER: That's very lucky they can carry your name. I've got nothing to carry my name.

MALCOLM: Where's this going?

ESTHER: I can't have children, Malcolm.

MALCOLM: What do you mean?

ESTHER: I'm getting too old.

MALCOLM: This is the first I've heard of you wanting children.

ESTHER: One child would be nice.

MALCOLM: You can have children.

ESTHER: I'm sorry, Malcolm, I've reached that age.

MALCOLM: Nonsense. Gee, look at you.

ESTHER: I've got no man and no child. If I'd had a child I'd have someone.

MALCOLM: You'll find a man.

ESTHER: I don't want to—I might be attractive to someone like you. That's just buying into loneliness.

MALCOLM: Relationships break down.

ESTHER: I didn't mind being your mistress for those years. Being a mistress is like marriage with the boring bits cut out. It's constant courting. But you did promise. On the old couch. You promised you'd leave your wife. You were firm about it, like everything else.

MALCOLM: I didn't promise.

Pause.

ESTHER: Don't condescend to me—

MALCOLM: I'm not—

ESTHER: Don't think a woman doesn't remember something like that.

Pause.

MALCOLM: The more you protest against the project, the more it costs me. The government won't give me permission because they think it'll lose them votes. But it's only you stopping it.

ESTHER: There are thousands of other people who agree with me.

MALCOLM: Because you're feeding them bullshit in order to get at me. The government's cowardice has meant that I'm paying a fortune, a huge fortune in interest rates every week on the bank's loans.

ESTHER: You have plenty of money.

MALCOLM: No, I'm completely over-stretched. I went out on a limb with this one—because it's so important. You just want to get at me—that's all it is.

ESTHER: Really? Or do I seriously believe in what I'm doing? You know why I got a new couch? The other was smelly. Stinking, actually. Once you broke off our relationship—oh, how well done was that? A meeting in a restaurant. I remember the words and your expression when I asked *why*? Oh, there was a sorry, or am I imagining it? And then a blur... Your hand on my back guiding me to a taxi. The last physical sensation of you. Very tender that hand, like guiding a sick woman... I remember embarrassing the taxi driver. I was weeping so much I couldn't tell him where I lived. Then I was back here, like magic. And I found myself standing here, in the middle of the room. How long was I standing here? I don't know. But it seemed as if I must have been in that pose for hours, because I felt as fragile as fine glass. If I moved I would shatter. And then I moved and broke. The good thing is that it's a blur. The carving knife on the floor. Why didn't I use it? Perhaps it was because I was too drunk. I was in the bed for days. I ate toast, nothing on it, that would have been too much trouble. For no reason at all I'd vomit, just where I stood. It'd be on my clothes and I didn't have the strength to change. Sometimes I'd look at my vomit and see a ring or piece of jewellery in it that you'd given me. Now, why would I try to swallow those things? What sort of madness is that? I didn't even have the strength to get off the couch, so I just pissed myself where I lay. Then I began to be aware of the mess this place was in. Things became less of a blur... and then the awful, awful feeling of loneliness. The loneliness. I've got no children like you, no relatives... It was like my blood had been changed into this fluid called loneliness and it flowed through every vein. You deserted me. You created that loneliness.

She slaps him across the face. Silence.

MALCOLM: Never do that to me again.

ESTHER: Hit me. Come on, hit me. Aren't you a man?

Silence.

MALCOLM: I'm dying.

She laughs.

I'm dying.

ESTHER: What sort of excuse is that?

MALCOLM: I have been given three, four months. I need to know that
it's going ahead. It's my biggest project. Yes, I am full of pride. This
development will be something to be proud of.

ESTHER: You'll be dead when it's done.

MALCOLM: My sons won't be.

ESTHER: Pride? It's vanity, Malcolm.

MALCOLM: I don't have much time.

ESTHER: I've run out of time too. My womb is dead.

MALCOLM: You never wanted children!

ESTHER: I didn't want loneliness! I'm going to come at you, Malcolm.
Yes, part of it is personal, but you will destroy a unique part of that
park—for your vanity. I won't stop, Malcolm, I won't shut up.

MALCOLM: You've changed. God, you've changed.

ESTHER: You made me like this. You created me. Look at me. I'm you.

◆ ◆ ◆ ◆ ◆

SCENE FOUR

Nightclub office. RAY *is cutting some cocaine on a glass tray.* LUKE *is
taking out an envelope.*

RAY: At this hour of the evening, a pick-me-up is in order. You agreeable
on this?

LUKE: I never took you for—

RAY: It is an over-demonised stimulant. My fee, I presume?

LUKE: Dad said you prefer cash.

RAY: Paper trails, Luke. Never make them. It's nice to have some lucre,
things are a bit tight at the moment. Bookmakers have no patience.
Your dad went on and on…

He sniffs some cocaine. Silence. He gestures for LUKE *to take some, which he does.*

… about that woman. It's now hitting my mucus ducts. Visualise it. I thought we solved the problem with the union boofhead. Incidentally, that fellow skedaddled up to Queensland. Must have put the fear of God into him.

VICTOR *enters.*

Victor! Luke, my sidekick Victor. Luke.

LUKE: Hello, Victor.

RAY: He handled the more unpleasant side effects of dealing with that unionist. Victor, the tray.

VICTOR *goes over to the tray to have some cocaine.*

LUKE: So how did you do that, Victor?

RAY: He can't hear you, Luke. He's deaf.

LUKE: Deaf, yeah, didn't hear me.

RAY *laughs.*

RAY: Tickling my mucus. Victor's deaf. But he has an uncanny way of reading lips. You'd never know he was stone deaf. The irony does not escape me, Luke. Here I am, the Sun King of the Underworld with a desire to be surrounded by dwarves, but my right-hand man is a deaf mute. All my bon mots literally fall onto deaf ears, Luke. He's highly sought after, is my Victor. You are highly sought after, aren't you Victor?

VICTOR: I am sought after.

RAY: Victor makes extra pocket money reading lips. Couple of years ago there was this big contretemps when that Australian fast bowler, McGrath, screamed abuse at some West Indian cricketer. No one knew what had been said, so a newspaper paid Victor to look at the video tapes and read their lips. Victor—the cricket—reading the lips.

VICTOR: I told them that when the West Indian cricketer Sarwan came to the crease, McGrath greeted him with, 'What does Brian Lara's cock taste like?' Sarwan's a young kid and loyal to his captain says—

RAY: Quick as a flash.

VICTOR: —quick as a flash Sarwan says, 'I don't know, ask your wife'. Then McGrath explodes, screaming, 'If you ever fucking mention my wife again, I'll cut your throat out'.

The three laugh. During the scene they sniff more cocaine, with the resultant effects.

RAY: So now the world knows what led up to McGrath's stream of obscenities—all due to Victor here. Take a bow, Victor. Oh yes, and Princess Diana. Tell him, Victor.

VICTOR: A writer showed me a videotape of Diana with her last boyfriend—the one she died with. They were talking in a car and he says to her, 'How about we go back to the hotel and have some more coke?' and she says, 'Then I'll give you the best blowjob of your life'.

RAY: Never made it into the biography. Victor got paid, though. I made sure of that. *Ay, caramba!* That's hit the spot. Your dad gets nervous.

LUKE: About what?

RAY: This woman, going on and on about how she's going to ruin him. We'll have a word to her. Do you have a girl, Luke?

LUKE: Not recently.

RAY: Anytime you're up for a frolic with one of the girls downstairs, just tell Uncle Ray. Victor, any time he wants to shag the talent, it's on the house. You can ask for anything, from the missionary position to the laplick to the freckle walkabout.

VICTOR: There's a new girl you might like—

RAY: Oh, Bettina, she gives rise to many concupiscent impulses. Not as good as Nikki, though. She was so accommodating that she's allowed me to fornicate with her doggy style so I could sniff cocaine off her back at the same time. Most of my girls are dykes. It's hard to get a girl who isn't a dyke or shop-soiled. My best strippers are dykes. They like to taunt men. And men believe they're interested in them. It's Percy that guides most men, Luke. The penis is like a hand puppet manipulated by a lunatic with the IQ of a cretin.

LUKE: You got a girl, you married?

RAY: Married once. Noelene. Lovely woman.

LUKE: How come you're still not with her, then?

RAY: Her obscene mouth during sexual congress.

LUKE: She was foul-mouthed?

RAY: Every time I was joying her—

LUKE: Joying her?

VICTOR *mimes sex with the index finger of one hand going into a circle created by the thumb and finger of his other hand.* LUKE *laughs.*

RAY: —she'd cry out the most obscene things. F-word this, c-word this... Really loud, waking up neighbours. Back me, Victor.

VICTOR: She had the mouth of a gutter.

LUKE: You heard her during sex?

VICTOR: Ray told me about it.

RAY: Now there's nothing I abhor more than a woman with a dirty mouth. I was totally offended by this. But the trouble is that I'm such a stallion that every time I joyed her, she orgasmed, and with it came all these four-letter words. She said she couldn't help it. Of course that foul tongue put me off—no satisfaction for Ray. Back me, Victor.

VICTOR: He'd come into work depressed.

RAY: Unfulfilled. So I stopped joying her. Naturally she was upset and left me. Since she's left me she's taken up with a parade of bastards and losers—acrobats, half a dozen bass players—I ask you, Luke, bass players? Liked the hunchback, though.

LUKE: You going to back him on that, Victor?

VICTOR: Excuse me, Luke.

LUKE: The hunchback.

VICTOR: Always bumping into things, couldn't see where he was going.

RAY: And then Coogan, the midget!

LUKE: Come on, that's—

RAY: Back me, Victor.

VICTOR: [*indicating*] This tall. Noelene said she was attracted to—

RAY: His disproportionate penis compared to the rest of him.

VICTOR: Coogan was trouble.

RAY: Yes, that midget was trouble. He took to Noelene with a cricket bat. You should have seen the bruises below her kneecaps. Thank God, he wasn't any taller. A nuisance personified. Noelene asked if I'd help her out, so Victor and I had to get rid of him. Jeez, he put up a struggle when we put him into the suitcase.

VICTOR: [*acting out*] Get in! Get in, you little fucker. Whoops, put that leg back in, shorty.

LUKE: What happened once you got him into the suitcase?

VICTOR: The train station.

RAY: We sent him to Dubbo as extra baggage. Never heard from him again. Women cause a lot of trouble even when they're victims. What is it about women, Luke? The power they have between their legs… if only they knew. We will not let this secret out of this room. But I could, Luke, leave this room, without opening a door.

LUKE: You can do that?

RAY: We humans are made up of atoms, so is that wall. It could be possible to merge into the atoms of the wall and then pass through onto the other side. One day that will be possible. As it will be possible to live forever.

LUKE: You want to live forever?

RAY: The idea of death is too frightening to contemplate. The idea of nothingness chills my heart. We will become atoms, we will become light.

LUKE: Are you going to back him on that, Victor?

VICTOR: She also said something else.

LUKE: Who?

VICTOR: Princess Di to her boyfriend. 'We can't have a baby if we continue to have sex the way you like.'

RAY: But nobody wants the truth.

VICTOR: Nobody wants the truth.

LUKE: What about you, Victor. Got a girl?

VICTOR *is busy sniffing some cocaine so he can't hear.*

RAY: Victor has been unlucky in love. He fell for a stripper called Jasmine. One of the best. What she did with foreign objects in her various orifices made grown men faint. She was only in love with booze. She'd drink perfume for the alcohol so her breath smelt good. Frangipani. Her DTs were something terrible to watch. Victor! Frangipani!

VICTOR *gives a mock melodramatic shiver.*

LUKE: You killed anyone, Victor?

VICTOR *doesn't hear.*

RAY: Victor's quite scary when he loses his temper.

LUKE: What about you?

RAY: In self defence. A few years ago one fellow, Ted Bone, he wanted to take over this club. He comes in, pulls out a revolver. At the time I'm showing one of the girls my new cockatoo—and he fires, but misses me. I take out my revolver and I shot him through the heart. Unfortunately, he stood up again and, boyo, that is a frightening thing to see. So I shoot him in the leg and still Boney comes at me, only this time he's got a limp. I shoot him again in the other leg, so he starts crawling towards me. A bullet through the forehead stopped him. Carked it at my feet. See, it was his nervous reactions that kept him going. It kind of traumatised the cockatoo. Until this day the only thing it can say is, '*Bang! Bang! Bang!*'

LUKE: Don't play with my mind, Ray.

RAY: Tomorrow, Luke, you'll enter my inner sanctum. I'll take you out back to my aviary. I have a grand collection of parrots and cockatoos.

LUKE *laughs.*

You love my parrots, don't you Victor? Victor? Victor? The parrots.

VICTOR: Ray teaches them to speak.

LUKE: What things?

VICTOR: Don't know. Parrots don't have lips. It's hard to read a beak. Impossible really.

RAY: Parrots tell you what you want to hear, unlike women.

VICTOR *laughs.*

What's so funny, Victor?

VICTOR: I'm as happy as a dog sniffing his best friend's arse.

LUKE: You don't like women, Ray?

RAY: The indignity of desire. Prone before the pudendum.

LUKE: Supine, you mean, supine.

RAY: So, it's happened to you too. They are very hard to talk to sometimes. But then sometimes women just need a good talking-to. Nicely, of course. Never heard your father more tense. Stressed.

LUKE: [*imitating a cockatoo*] Bang! Bang! Bang!

RAY: Bang! Bang! That's the spirit! I'm going to let you in on a little secret, Luke. Succulence. Succulence is all.

LUKE: Thanks, Ray.

RAY: I mean it. How to win over politicians and cops—give them the same thing: free drinks, free pussy, the usual frolics. Oh, and one more piece of advice—never bet on anything that has a jockey.

LUKE: But you do.

Things are high-pitched now, so RAY *decides to change the mood. He hits a remote control that operates a hidden sound system.*

RAY: Well, I speak from experience. Hare-brained Victor was once a hairdresser. Victor! He teaches the strippers their routines. There's a touch of the inner nancy in Victor. He can feel the music through the floor. I taught him this. My favourite. Victor, one, two three…

VICTOR *picks up a bottle, pretending it's a microphone, and starts miming to Billie Holiday singing 'You Don't Know What Love Is'. As he mimes,* RAY *and* LUKE *sniff more cocaine. There is something feminine about the performance. At the end, both men are moved by* VICTOR's *performance.*

Time to use your charm, Luke. You have to speak to that woman.

♦ ♦ ♦ ♦ ♦

SCENE FIVE

Esther's apartment. Day. LUKE *enters, followed by* ESTHER.

LUKE: I'm glad you'd talk to me, let alone invite me in.

ESTHER: Why shouldn't I? A drink.

LUKE: [*motioning*] Some of that?

ESTHER: Straight.

LUKE: Yes, I am. [*Pause.*] You look different from the pictures in the papers.

ESTHER: How so?

LUKE: Better in the flesh.

ESTHER: Did you have lessons in charm at your private school?

LUKE: I was a natural.

ESTHER: You look different from your photographs, too.

LUKE: What photographs?

ESTHER: That big magazine story on your family.

LUKE: So how do I come across?

ESTHER: Sweet in the photographs, in the flesh… conceited, charming, facile.

LUKE: Whoa, that's too much praise. [*Taking his drink*] Thank you.

ESTHER *has a drink too.*

A toast.

ESTHER: To what?

LUKE: Friendship.

ESTHER: Friendship?

LUKE: Really, we should be enemies.

ESTHER: To the best of enemies.

LUKE: To the best of enemies.

Pause.

ESTHER: Did your father send you here?

LUKE: God, no. I don't think he'd like that. What are all those caviar tins doing there?

ESTHER: That's my shrine. The man in the photograph is my father. He imported caviar. Those caviar tins are empty, but they're the most famous brands—from Russia to Iran. Of course, you can't bring in the quantities that you used to—the sturgeon is being hunted to extinction. Do you like caviar, Luke?

LUKE: I had it once, but then I found out how they deal with the sturgeon. To get the eggs you cut open her belly while she's still alive to collect the roe as quickly as possible.

ESTHER: That's because once she's dead, her body releases a chemical substance that harms the eggs. I thought most men would like the idea of ravaging a female body while she's half dead. Did you like the taste?

LUKE: It was so-so.

ESTHER: Then you didn't have the best. By the age of nine, I had tasted all the best caviar in the world. My father took me to all those places from big freezers in Russia to rotting quays in Azerbaijan.

LUKE: Ever cut open a living sturgeon yourself?

ESTHER: Yes. A small one.

LUKE: You taste her eggs?

ESTHER: No, they have to go through a long process, including being salted. Go on, get to it. The reason why you're here.

Pause.

LUKE: I'm sure you know.

ESTHER: Your father didn't send you?

LUKE: He doesn't know I'm here. You certainly know how to get good press.

ESTHER: I used to be a journalist. I know how the media works.

LUKE: You're not anymore?

ESTHER: I've been a lady of leisure for a few years.

LUKE: Your dad left you with a large inheritance?

ESTHER: A small one, and then for a few years I've been a kept woman.

LUKE: A mistress?

ESTHER: That's a common word. But yes.

LUKE: Are you still one?

ESTHER: That's a bit rude.

LUKE: Given that you seem to know a lot about my family—I think I can be rude. How did you know that my father agreed for Todd to come back into the business?

ESTHER: A little birdie told me.

LUKE: When I was young my mother said a woman's private parts were called a Little Birdie. So, a talking vagina told you?

Pause.

ESTHER: You think a charming manner and smile can allow you to be vulgar.

LUKE: Sometimes. The thing is that you are using all sorts of personal details about us to make people hate the Boyce family.

ESTHER: I didn't need to do that. Your father is regarded as a very domineering man.

LUKE: In our business you have to bully and push, or else the opposition will destroy you.

ESTHER: You don't strike me as a bully.

LUKE: I'm in training.

Pause.

ESTHER: You won't change my mind. The development stinks—

LUKE: This Hesperus thing could break us.

ESTHER: I heard through the grapevine that your brother Keith opposes it.

LUKE: He thinks we still have time to pull out, but my father wants to go ahead—it would be our most major project.

ESTHER: And you're supporting your father in all of this?

LUKE: I like risk. So does he.

ESTHER: So you have something in common.

> LUKE *holds out his drink. She takes it and goes to pour him another one.*

LUKE: He wants this to be his monument.

ESTHER: He wants to create a dynasty. That's all.

LUKE: Don't we all?

ESTHER: If you've got kids to pass it on to. That's why he brought Todd back into the fold, isn't it—because his girlfriend is having a baby?

LUKE: You sure you don't have listening devices in our home.

Susie Lindeman as Esther and Toby Schmitz as Luke in the 2005 Griffin Theatre Company production of THE MARVELLOUS BOY. *(Photo: Robert McFarlane)*

ESTHER: You're still living at home?

LUKE: Mum wants me there. It's a big place to be in by yourself.

ESTHER: Yes, we've all heard about your father paying an obscene amount of money for Beauchamp. A bit over-the-top, the renovation. A brothel feel to some of the rooms.

LUKE: [*taking the drink*] Thank you. You've seen inside it?

ESTHER: Those pictures in the magazine.

LUKE: My mother likes plushness. And if brothels are plush—and who am I to know what the interior of brothels look like—then Beauchamp's insides are plush.

ESTHER: You love your mother.

LUKE: Of course.

ESTHER: What I've learnt is that a woman should never become involved with a man who hated his mother.

LUKE: So, I get a tick. Did you have an affair with Bain Cipolla?

ESTHER: An affair?

LUKE: A bit of joying with him.

ESTHER: Joying?

LUKE: An expression that a friend uses. Cipolla and you. I found out that his union was willing to give up the picket months before they did, but he kept on pressuring his members to keep it up. All the time you were giving him information about us.

ESTHER: And what makes you think I would have done something so…?

LUKE: Calculating…? Because this attack on the project seems to be personal and taking up all your life. Why not keep Cipolla enthralled?

ESTHER: [*amused*] Enthralled? I don't think I can enthrall anybody.

LUKE: I think it would be easy for you.

   Pause.

ESTHER: You're very good. Very good. Slick Luke.

LUKE: Don't, I'm embarrassed, stop praising me.

ESTHER: You think you're that good.

LUKE: About what?

ESTHER: You can't stop me in one way, so you decide to woo me in another. My heart's a-flutter, flutter… All right, I'll give up my campaign. Flutter, flutter.

LUKE: Sarcasm becomes you.

Silence.

ESTHER: You won't stop me, Luke.

He downs the last of his drink.

LUKE: Thank you.

ESTHER: I've enjoyed this little talk. I always wondered what you'd be like.

LUKE: Impressed?

ESTHER: Not very. The last card wasn't a terribly good one to play.

LUKE: I didn't mean it like that.

ESTHER: Oh, come on, Luke.

Pause.

LUKE: I was telling you the truth. You are attractive. I can understand why Bain Cipolla almost ruined his union because of you. Thank you for the caviar lesson. I might try it again.

ESTHER: Yes. It's the thrill of knowing the eggs came from her while she was alive that gives the best caviar its special taste.

LUKE *goes.* ESTHER *sips her drink, lost in contemplation.*

SCENE SIX

Aviary, late afternoon. VICTOR, *wearing sunglasses, has been feeding the parrots.* RAY *enters with* LUKE.

RAY: Not many people get to see my parrots, Luke. So you should feel privileged.

LUKE: Anytime I'm with you I feel privileged, Ray.

RAY: I can understand that feeling. How's Denis, Victor? Victor! How's Denis?

VICTOR: He's eating again.

RAY: [*pointing out a bird to* LUKE] A Major Mitchell. Clever as they come. [*Pointing elsewhere*] That, now that is rare.

VICTOR: Sheila.

RAY: An eclectus parrot. Female. Hence the scarlet feathers with that lovely blue band on the lower breast. What I want is the night parrot… but it's rare. But they could still be alive. One was found dead by a road in outback Queensland a decade or so ago. That Nancy over there. What a temper. What a temper, eh, Victor? Hate to be her husband. This Esther woman… she common?

LUKE: No.

RAY: Not common?

LUKE: Uncommon.

RAY: [*motioning to the parrot*] My favourite paraquito. What else about her?

LUKE: Intelligent. Committed to her cause.

RAY: How committed?

LUKE: I don't know.

RAY: Women can be… bloody-minded, like Nancy here. Just for the hell of it. So if I suddenly arrived on her front door—

LUKE: I don't think confrontation would do the job, Ray.

RAY: That is not the way I do things, Luke. Do you want to have another crack at her?

LUKE: I think softly does it is the best way with her.

RAY: Was she joying that Cipolla fellow to keep him on-side?

LUKE: In all likelihood.

RAY: If she does something like that, it means she's playing for keeps. Victor, there's no seed in that cage. Seed? Doesn't matter. I'll get it.

  RAY *goes.*

VICTOR: Where's Ray going?

LUKE: To get some seed. [*Pause.*] This is some collection, Victor.

VICTOR: Yes, Ray's been collecting them for years. He loves them, more than humans, I think. He even kisses them on the beaks… disgusting, to my mind. They have all sorts of diseases. I tell him and he says to me, 'Victor, humans carry more diseases than parrots'. He's been a bit concerned lately about them.

LUKE: What's the problem?

VICTOR: He may have to get rid of the nightclub—and that means his aviary will have to go, too.

LUKE: Why will he have to get rid of it?

VICTOR: The nightclub? Well, you look at it. It used to look the best, now… See, Ray was once very rich. Made a fortune bringing out rock-and-roll bands. But he hated rock-and-roll. 'Not one of those talentless twerps knows an augmented chord,' he says over and over. And he hated how the girls would scream and cry in the concerts and piss themselves with excitement. He said the cleaning bills for the venues were astronomical. He loves jazz. He brought out the best, but no one came to see them and, given most were junkies, he was spending a fortune on their heroin habits. Lost a fortune. He clung on to this club. But he needs to do side projects to keep his head above water. Like your dad. Your dad always pays right on time. Cash.

LUKE: How did you two get together?

VICTOR: I was a bouncer when he started out and he took a shining to me, he said. He said we were the two musketeers. He even said I could share Noelene.

LUKE: His wife? He didn't mind?

VICTOR: He said his mind was on other things. He's a bit of a loner.

LUKE: I guess when he was in the orphanage he didn't make friends.

VICTOR: He wasn't in an orphanage. I was the one brought up in an orphanage. His mum brought him up after his dad died. She just died recently herself.

LUKE: So the story about being brought up in a Catholic orphanage is a lie?

VICTOR: Oh, yes. He has a brilliant ability to tell the right lies to people. He says it puts him at an advantage.

LUKE: What about his wife and the midget?

VICTOR: Oh, all that's true. I think Noelene gets involved with real bastards so he'll come and rescue her.

LUKE: She must still love him.

VICTOR: Oh, yes, when he sent her to my room for the first time all she did was cry all night. Thank goodness, I'm deaf, or else I could have got real jack of her. You fix up this Esther woman, Luke. [*Pause.*] What you have to understand about Ray, is that you have to stay on his good side.

LUKE: What's his bad side like?

VICTOR: Cold as ice. So don't get frostbitten.

RAY *enters.*

RAY: Who's going to get frostbitten?

LUKE: Victor told me to avoid it.

RAY: Sensible Victor.

He throws a bag of seed at VICTOR *who catches it.*

Darling's cage. Are you enjoying yourself, Luke?

LUKE: Out here? Yeah, I like the parrots.

RAY: No, I mean, the general experience of being within my orbit.

LUKE: Very much, Ray.

RAY: You mean it?

LUKE: I mean it.

RAY: You know, time is of the essence, *vis-a-vis* your father's problems.

LUKE: I am aware of that, Ray.

RAY: I'm keeping from your father the fact that you're dealing with this woman.

LUKE: I am too.

RAY: She attractive, this Esther?

LUKE: Yes.

RAY: For her age, judging by her photographs, she seems to still be holding up rather well... Any man in her life?

LUKE: She used to be a mistress to some guy, but they broke up.

RAY: She's alone?

LUKE: I think so.

RAY: Lonely?

LUKE: She has a facade that's hard to crack.

RAY: You'll just have to peek behind the facade, then. And, my dear boy, keep what you're doing with her from your father. Surprise him when you win her over.

He gives LUKE *a small paper bag of seed.*

This is even a greater honour for me to bestow. You can feed those rainbow lorikeets. [*Pause.*] You just say the word if you need my help.

LUKE: I won't need your help.

RAY: I'll determine whether you need my help or not... Understand me, Luke?

♦ ♦ ♦ ♦ ♦

SCENE SEVEN

Esther's house. Afternoon. Gradually we are aware that ESTHER *is speaking to* LUKE.

ESTHER: Sometimes he thought he was lying next to a ghost. He would look across at her pale face and think she was not breathing, as if she were in a state of suspended animation. The heat did not seem to affect her, whereas he was constantly bathed in a sheen of perspiration. Sometimes he would doze off but she never seemed to sleep and remained engrossed in her own thoughts of which he could only guess at. He never questioned this ritual for fear of somehow tampering with its mystery and the intimacy of their days and nights.

What had intrigued him from his very first visit were six dresses hanging from the wall. They ranged from the severe to the flamboyant and he had the feeling, rightly or wrongly, that they meant so much to her that if she were to wear one then her behaviour would change in accordance with it. He pointed to a 1940s green silk dress. It was perhaps the least flamboyant but the material was so exquisite, the colour so ravishing that the thought it was one of the most elegant dresses he had ever seen. 'It's my mother's,' she said.

A few days later she rang to tell him that her mother was dying and she would have to spend much of her time with her, but this didn't mean that they should stop seeing one another. One evening when he arrived she was wearing the green dress. Without a word she grabbed his hand and guided him to the bed. They didn't make love but merely lay together on the bed—he naked and she next to him in her silk dress that flowed over her body like a green river. For hours they said nothing, but she was comforted by his presence and, in turn, he was comforted by her unexplainable behaviour.

The ritual continued through the sultry summer. Whenever she was not at the hospital caring for her mother he would visit her. When he arrived she would be wearing the green dress, and without a word he would take off his clothes and they would lie on the bed together. Occasionally she would talk about her dying mother and in a guilty manner say, 'There were times when I hated her, but I always loved her'. Sometimes she would say nothing and put her head on his shoulder and he was shocked by how cold her skin felt.

He had been with many women in his life but she had affected him more deeply than had any other, and yet he didn't know the reason why. Five weeks later the mother died. She asked him to come to the funeral. He was late. There were a few dozen mourners, none of whom he knew, and he joined the end of the line that was filing past the open coffin where his lover stood, dress not in black but in defiant white, her face radiant with grief. He hated anything to do with death but was curious to see the mother because he had no idea what she looked like.

The line moved slowly as some mourners paused to whisper goodbye to the dead woman or kiss her forehead. Finally, he reached the coffin and was startled to see that the corpse was wearing the green dress. What was even more unsettling for him was that her make-up and hair was exactly like that of her daughter. Even her peaceful expression was the same as her daughter's when she lay on the bed next to him during those days and nights of waiting for the mother to die. It was almost as if the daughter had become her mother, or was it the other way round?

Not aware of what he was doing, he bent over the coffin and kissed the corpse on the mouth. As he stood up, his lips red from the dead mother's lipstick, he glanced across at the daughter who blushed, not with embarrassment but with desire, something he had never seen in her before. At that moment he realised that now her mother was dead, she would reveal her innermost self to him. Later, as she talked to some mourners, he silently slipped away without saying goodbye. She never saw him again.

Silence.

LUKE: Why did he do that?

ESTHER: He fell in love with her mystery. Not her.

LUKE: And that's the first story you wrote.

ESTHER: That's it. My only story. I was so proud of it. I used to remember every single word.

LUKE: Was it published?

ESTHER: No, because no one knew why he left her. Too obscure. So I took up journalism. It taught me to think clearly and to write simply.

LUKE: But you don't do that anymore.

ESTHER: My hands are full-stopping the Boyces. Which is why you're
here.

LUKE: A social visit.

ESTHER: Come on, Luke.

LUKE: It's the truth. I don't want to talk about Hesperus Park.

ESTHER: You seem creative. Did you ever want to be a writer, too?

LUKE: No. I did create a comic once. It was about a teenage superhero.
I called it *Bipolar Boy*. When he was in his manic phase he cleaned
up all the criminal elements in the city, fought corruption tirelessly,
but he annoyed people because he was filling up the prisons, but
when he was depressed he'd just lie in bed while criminals went
berserk. The city put him on medication. Because he was happy
and contented, he just watched TV all day. When the city asked him
to clean up the gangsters he'd just say, 'Hey man, just chill out'. I
think I got a good grade for it.

ESTHER: Did you write it because of your epilepsy?

> *Pause.*

LUKE: How do you know about that?

ESTHER: The talking vagina.

LUKE: Can hardly wait to hear it.

ESTHER: But you don't suffer from it anymore? [*Pause.*] You seem
uncomfortable.

LUKE: You seem to know much more about me than I do about you.

ESTHER: There's not much to tell. What causes the fits?

LUKE: Various theories. Stuffed-up electrical wiring in the head. Pressure.
Stress.

ESTHER: Do you know you're having them?

LUKE: No. After you have them it's like waking up really tired. There's
a feeling that you're watching yourself. I watch myself watching
myself.

ESTHER: If you had one now what would I do?

LUKE: Step away. Watch. [*Smiling*] You could watch me. That's the only
photograph in the house. You must have loved your dad very much.

ESTHER: I used to dream of him being inside me and I'd spew him up,
like ectoplasm, and he'd form in front of me—become real again.

Sometimes I sit in front of a piece of blank paper with a pencil and let him direct my hand, so he writes messages to me.

LUKE: A ghost?

ESTHER: A presence, like at night when you walk into a spider's web. It's weightless but you can feel it on your face.

LUKE: So you believe in the afterlife?

ESTHER: I have to. It's the only way you can keep hold of your loved ones. Life wouldn't make sense otherwise.

LUKE: The man who kept you—he was older?

ESTHER: [*laughing*] Of course. Although the word 'kept'...

LUKE: He was a nice man?

ESTHER: He started out that way. I mean, who can tell with men? At the time when my father was dying, I had a boyfriend who didn't want to have sex with me, but on the night of my father's funeral he was gung-ho for it.

LUKE: So did you?

ESTHER: Very personal. No. I thought the symbolism was too crass. Thantos and Eros.

LUKE: What happened to this recent fellow—the older guy?

ESTHER: Why do you want to know?

LUKE: I'm a very curious person.

ESTHER: I got tired of him. Don't you have a girlfriend?

LUKE: I thought you knew everything about me. I wouldn't be here if I did.

    Pause.

ESTHER: You're good, Luke.

LUKE: As in?

ESTHER: The dance you do. The dance you're doing around me. [*Pause.*] I have to go to a public meeting where I'm going to slag the Boyces.

LUKE: What about?

ESTHER: This time it's the design.

LUKE: That is regarded as a brilliant design.

ESTHER: An architect's wet dream. All out of sympathy with the environment of the place. Your dad should have told him to tone it down.

LUKE: You ever dealt with architects? In every architect beats the heart of a fascist. Dad made sure he got the best architect. You know we're known for cheap and affordable housing. This is a project that Dad believes will stop people looking down on us.

ESTHER: Maybe he should have kept to cheap and affordable housing.

LUKE: Too late to turn back now.

ESTHER: No, it isn't.

Pause.

LUKE: What time is this meeting?

ESTHER: Are you going to it?

LUKE: No. What time?

ESTHER: Couple of hours. [*Pause.*] You can't get at me, Luke. You see, I've never had a belief, a purpose before. I like feeling I have a purpose.

LUKE: I have no intention of changing your beliefs.

ESTHER: Do you believe in anything, Luke? Do you believe in fucking anything?

LUKE: I believe in this project.

ESTHER: If your father wasn't involved, would you?

LUKE: I don't know.

ESTHER: There you are.

LUKE: I'm glad you're confident that I'd never change your convictions. Because that means I can ask what I'm going to—and you can be sure it's nothing to do about Hesperus Park.

ESTHER: What's it got to do with, then?

LUKE: I have a test for you.

He pulls a jar from out of a bag, a bottle of vodka, two shot glasses and a spoon.

I bought some caviar. It's a taste test.

ESTHER: And that?

LUKE: I'm told that vodka shots are essential with it.

He gives her the jar of caviar and the small spoon.

ESTHER: A wooden spoon.

LUKE: I was told that a silver spoon alters the taste. My research true?

She laughs and nods. While he pours them both some vodka, ESTHER tastes the caviar and savours it for a long time. He gives her a shot of vodka which she immediately swallows.

Well?

ESTHER: Did you taste it?

LUKE: Not yet.

ESTHER: Take my spoon.

He has a spoonful and then a shot of vodka.

What do you think?

LUKE: Yes, nutty… it's like the eggs bust open and realise their flavour on your tongue. It's a beautiful taste…

ESTHER: So it should be—it's Osetra from the *Acipenser gueldenstaedti*. Smaller grained than Beluga and better tasting. Did I pass?

LUKE: Top marks.

They continue to dip into the caviar and drink shots of vodka.

Perhaps the innards of a half-dead, gutted female are exquisite after all. Besides being a mistress, did you ever have a long-term relationship?

ESTHER: You're buying my personal secrets with this very expensive caviar.

LUKE: I don't know about buying them.

ESTHER: I was always afraid I'd make a mistake. When I was nineteen I fell hopelessly in love with a married man. We went off for a dirty weekend. He was rowing me across a lake when a storm came up. He started to panic and at that moment I realised I didn't love him. And as lightning and thunder came closer I thought, 'What if a lightning bolt kills us and they discover our bodies and think that even right up until the last moment I loved him?'

LUKE *laughs. They are getting tipsy.*

You have a nice laugh.

LUKE: Your first compliment.

ESTHER: I'm sure I've made others. So, I've made sure I've never gone rowing with another man.

LUKE: You seem to have a thing for married men.

ESTHER: A habit. Notice the slightly nutty flavour.

LUKE: [*savouring the caviar*] Yes.

ESTHER: The first time I tasted Osetra I was in Russia. All of seventeen years old. The son of a wealthy exporter was keen on me. He fed it to me—as if wanting to make me drunk on caviar.

LUKE: Did it make you drunk?

ESTHER: That plus the vodka.

LUKE: He get his way?

ESTHER: He wasn't old enough for me, then.

LUKE: So he did.

ESTHER: Did you have many girlfriends when you were young?

LUKE: The usual, I suppose.

ESTHER: Anyone manage to get under your skin?

LUKE: One girl. She was an oboe player like me. We went on a European tour with the university orchestra. It was quite an affair, but the moment we got back to Sydney she dropped me.

ESTHER: What did you do?

LUKE: Sold my oboe.

ESTHER: In that magazine profile of your family you have a very lovely smile.

LUKE: Every single photograph of me since I was born—I'm always smiling. Happy.

ESTHER: Unlike your brothers?

LUKE: I'm the youngest—we always get the best of everything.

ESTHER: Given to you, like on a platter?

LUKE: If that were so, how come you're not on my platter?

ESTHER *laughs. Pause.*

ESTHER: I want to tell you about the married guy I was involved with.

LUKE: I don't want to know. I'm already jealous of that Russian.

Pause.

ESTHER: I am not prey, Luke.

LUKE: Prey?

ESTHER: Lonely woman, I'm not.

LUKE: I've never thought you are.

ESTHER: I can look after myself very well. Much better than you think. Do you think I'm flattered by the attentions of someone younger, like you?

LUKE: I'm kind of hoping you'll be godsmacked.

ESTHER: [*with a laugh*] Godsmacked. What if I'm not?

LUKE: Then you'll have to give me another opportunity.

ESTHER: Do these lines work on other women?

LUKE: I've never tried them before. [*Pause.*] I want you.

Silence.

ESTHER: The position is this: I'm going to take you.

◆◆◆◆◆

SCENE EIGHT

Ray's office. Afternoon. VICTOR, *wearing hair-tint-stained rubber gloves, is finishing dyeing and trimming* RAY's *hair. He is talking as* RAY *is engrossed in reading a newspaper item.*

VICTOR: I went through the accounts again. It's the second week we've lost money. We have to do something about this, Ray. Maybe the girls are too skinny. Maybe we need healthy-looking girls. That Nikki is a strange one. The one with the excellent make-up. She was telling me that when she does bucks' parties she only allows the guys to do it doggy style so it doesn't mess up her make-up. I can understand that. It does take her hours to get her face right. Why have some drunken buck slobber all over it? You don't think Sharon's getting a little long in the tooth, do you, Ray—?

RAY: [*not looking up from the newspaper*] She works for half what the other girls do. It's a saving. Tell her to shave off her pubic hair, it'll take years off her.

LUKE *enters.*

LUKE: Saving on money, Ray?

RAY: I told you Victor trained as a hairdresser. It saves me from going to a barber. That would be a dreadful way to die. A barber slitting your throat as you sit in a chair. A long time dying, I suspect.

LUKE: It's looking rather empty downstairs.

RAY: Couple of the girls called in sick. I'll have to find some new girls. Girls on heroin don't make good pole dancers—that requires coordination and muscle power. Junkies make good lap dancers. Now, this is an interesting article—scientists are rethinking the avian brain. To call someone a birdbrain, is considered a put-down, but really birds have very sharp brains. Not only do crows make hooks and spears of small sticks to carry on foraging expeditions, some have learnt to put walnuts on roads for cars to crack. African grey parrots not only talk, they have a sense of humour and make up new words. Baby songbirds babble like human infants, using the left sides of their brains. Victor, we must get an African grey parrot. Now, my boy, I wanted to see you.

LUKE: That's why I'm here.

RAY: This Esther female: how's it going?

LUKE: Fine.

RAY: Fine? Fine, like the weather?

LUKE: Fine as in, she likes me and I'm beginning to win her over.

RAY: Beginning? I was hoping you'd be further down the track with her.

LUKE: She's a very determined woman.

RAY: Your father thinks she's unstable. [*Pause.*] Luke, Luke, don't let me down on this. I get tired of seeing her face in the papers—it's even in there today. Is she a birdbrain?

LUKE: In the new sense of the term—yes.

RAY: I notice a spring in your step. I was hoping I was the cause, but I detect another reason—you are joying this Esther. You know a woman is falling for you if she allows you backyard prospecting rights—have you got them yet? [*Pause.*] I like you, Luke, you're like the son I never had. I know you're on a learning curve, but it's about time you went in a straight line. Now, your dad rang me this morning. He was on his way to the hospital for chemo. He stops at the traffic lights and thinks, 'Bugger it, no more chemo for me. It only makes me sicker.'

LUKE: He's stopping it?

RAY: It's what he tells me. Chemo gives him an extra month or so, but it makes him nauseous—can't think.

LUKE: But it gives him time.

RAY: He says he's living in a haze. That's not making use of time. I understand his predicament. He needs to be on his toes. So, Luke, time is of the essence. He was upset by selective quotes from some nut's architectural report in this morning's paper.

LUKE: The academic?

RAY: Obviously Esther paid him.

VICTOR: What would a fucking academic know about the real world?

RAY: Precisely, Victor. Some girls who work here are students... They say, to a woman, that academics are obsessed with ejaculation onto their faces.

LUKE: [*sardonically*] Really?

RAY: Would they have a reason to lie, Luke? Back me, Victor.

VICTOR: Ray calls if facial spoilage.

RAY: Because of this time factor, Luke, your father will double the money if I get this woman off his back, asap. She's got a vendetta against your father. So, in return, we have a vendetta against her. I always deliver. I pride myself on that. The matter is of some urgency.

    Pause.

LUKE: Did you tell him I'm dealing with Esther?

RAY: It can be a surprise once you convince her. You see, this is the problem, Luke. You have a couple of days to win her over, to stop her blabbermouthing. She must stop this campaign.

LUKE: It's going to be—

RAY: Easy! Luke, I'm rather keen to get that money your father has promised me. I've got several persistent bookmakers wanting to speak to me—and I don't like the tone in their voices.

VICTOR: Your mum wants to speak to you.

LUKE: What?

RAY: Your dad told me. He tried to call you but your mobile's off.

LUKE: About what?

RAY: The wedding. Your mother doesn't want you to ad lib your speech. She wants you to write it down.

LUKE: She wants to check it?

RAY: Well, if I were her, I'd say the same thing. You know how smart-arse you can be.

LUKE: I'll give her a call later.

VICTOR: Never keep your mother waiting, Luke.

RAY: If you can't convince Esther, then Uncle Ray will have to do it. Back me, Victor.

VICTOR: Ray is a very good convincer.

                    ♦ ♦ ♦ ♦ ♦

SCENE NINE

Esther's living room. Evening. ESTHER *comes out of the bedroom wearing a kimono.*

ESTHER: [*calling back into the bedroom*] Isn't what we did illegal in some American states?

LUKE: [*entering from the bedroom*] I hope so. I'd like to think that every time I make love to you I break the law. [*Licking his fingers*] I don't know where the caviar ends and you begin.

She kisses and sucks his fingers.

ESTHER: You're becoming quite a connoisseur of caviar.

LUKE: Yes, that's what I thought too. And that—

ESTHER: Yes, I'm going to pour some.

She pours some wine for the two of them.

LUKE: [*re: the photograph*] Your father's ghost, would he approve?

ESTHER: I'll have to ask him.

LUKE: Would he have liked me?

ESTHER: Oh, he was charming and light-hearted, too.

LUKE: That's a yes? [*Pause.*] Now, are you godsmacked?

ESTHER: I enjoy it.

LUKE: Is that all?

ESTHER: You must be careful of your vanity, Luke.

LUKE: It's nothing to do with that. [*Pause.*] I don't like this being only an occasional thing.

Pause.

ESTHER: Don't do this to me, Luke.

LUKE: I'm doing nothing. I want you to know.

ESTHER: I made a mistake. I should never have embarked on this.

LUKE: Why?

ESTHER: Is this how badly you want to win?

LUKE: I don't want to win. I want you.

Pause.

ESTHER: I should never... You're not the vain one, I am. And why should I be vain? I'm much older than you, Luke, so please, let's just keep it as a bit of nookie. Nothing more.

LUKE: I can't. I think about you all the time—

ESTHER: Your father... think about him.

LUKE: Well, I'd hate to be thinking about him in the way I think about you.

ESTHER: You can't play both sides of the fence. Are you still toying with me?

LUKE: I am not toying with you. My father can look after himself.

ESTHER: I thought he was dying?

LUKE: But you're living.

ESTHER: Whose side are you on?

LUKE: Mine. Yours. My father's. My brothers'.

ESTHER: You have to choose. I'm not going to give up my campaign.

LUKE: I don't want you to. I'm going to tell my father what's happening.

ESTHER: Don't.

LUKE: I don't particularly like hiding what I feel for you from him.

ESTHER: You will bitterly disappoint him if you tell him what's been happening. He'll regard it as betrayal. You know that. [*Pause.*] For God's sake, get a woman your own age.

LUKE: Never tell me that. Never.

ESTHER: Mr Bossy Boots now.

LUKE: I hate this feeling. I hate this feeling of being out of control. You know, you can do anything to me. Anything you like, as long as you'll be with me.

ESTHER: Don't go on with this.

LUKE: Can't help it. I want you.

Silence.

ESTHER: Oh, Luke. Why are you doing this to me?

LUKE: Because you're doing this to me. I have never wanted anybody like I want you. I have never felt this way in my life. To put no finer point on it, Esther, I am love-struck, cunt-struck, awestruck.

Pause.

ESTHER: Nobody's ever told me that before.

Silence.

LUKE: How about it, luv?

ESTHER: How about what?

LUKE: Everything.

He moves to kiss her.

ESTHER: Stay away. Just back… just a bit away, let me breathe. [*Pause.*] Luke, please don't do this to me. You have complicated everything. [*Pause.*] You are supposed to be protecting your family's interests.

LUKE: I did come here the first time with the aim of changing your mind. Now I don't care.

ESTHER: Your father doesn't know you're doing this? Was this your own initiative?

LUKE: Yes.

ESTHER: Why not your brothers'?

LUKE: Todd's busy getting married and Keith thinks we're too financially stretched to do the project.

ESTHER: So Keith's the sensible one?

LUKE: The conservative one.

ESTHER: What if I don't change my mind?

LUKE: Then that's the way it's going to be.

Pause.

ESTHER: Jesus Christ. [*Pause.*] I am a very difficult woman, Luke.

LUKE: I want a complicated woman. That way it's not boring.

ESTHER: That smile—that is too damn fucking infectious.

LUKE: You know I love you. Do you love me?

Pause.

ESTHER: I don't know. I told you I was difficult.

LUKE: Well, I'm going to wait until you tell me you do.

♦ ♦ ♦ ♦ ♦

SCENE TEN

Luke's office. Day. He is finishing wrapping a present as MALCOLM *enters.*

MALCOLM: Mind if I come in?

LUKE: 'Course not.

MALCOLM: [*surveying the office*] This office is rather small, isn't it?

LUKE: You're the boss, you've got the big one.

MALCOLM: A wedding gift?

LUKE: No, a present. I'm going out with this girl…

MALCOLM: Is she nice?

LUKE: Very special.

MALCOLM: You're serous about this one?

LUKE: Very.

MALCOLM: When can I meet her?

LUKE: I thought I'd wait until Todd's hitched.

MALCOLM: You think of marrying this girl?

LUKE: It's crossed my mind. [*Pause.*] You're looking well.

MALCOLM: Some mornings I can hardly believe I'm dying. Other mornings I wake up thinking I'm dead. You must be careful about this girl.

LUKE: What do you mean?

MALCOLM: Marriage is very… Well, you know how me and your mum have had our ups and downs.

LUKE: I think it's called a roller coaster.

MALCOLM: Women can be… different.

LUKE: [*with a laugh*] I hope so.

MALCOLM: The trouble with a woman is that you can never tell when she's mad or not. You can tell when a man goes mad, but never with a woman. You just think she's having a bad month. A man would never go through a woman's private things, but your mother has always gone through my drawers. She denies it, but I know. They can never separate the private from the public. That's what we do. That's what you must do. What do you think of Ray?

LUKE: Underneath all that bluster is a good guy, I think.

MALCOLM: He's a necessary evil.

LUKE: I haven't seen the evil.

MALCOLM: That's probably the wrong word. You'll probably need him for a while. Once this project gets up and running it won't be the end of our troubles. The unions will want to push us—test our patience, see what they can get away with. You'll have to know where to draw the line and tell them if they cross it then they're dead meat. Local councillors will want kickbacks or else they'll hinder us all the way. Politicians… jeez… you know what Ray says: 'Politicians are God's punishment for our belief in the essential goodness of humanity'. He's right. You be tough like Ray. Like me. Understand that?

LUKE: Of course.

MALCOLM: There's no of course about it. Either you do...

LUKE: I do.

MALCOLM: If you're not, people will take advantage of you and your brothers.

LUKE: I will do right by you.

Pause.

MALCOLM: Do you admire me?

LUKE: Yes, I admire what you've done.

MALCOLM: Some things I've done... I've done for the right reasons, but I've had to do them in a way that others would find dubious.

LUKE: Ray's a dubious thing?

MALCOLM: Yes. If you don't impose yourself on life, Luke, it will impose itself on you. [*Pause.*] Tomorrow there will be a full-page ad in most of the papers explaining our position. You know how the protesters have lied and got everything wrong. It's a huge cost. Really it's a final card, but the bankers are after us to do something positive. Get the public to see the project from our point of view.

LUKE: How close are we to going under?

MALCOLM: Chest-deep and the waves are coming in. So the next few days are crucial. Life or death, really. So what's the problem about tonight?

LUKE What do you mean?

MALCOLM: Todd said you weren't going to his bucks' night.

LUKE: A bucks' night is not on the top of my agenda of favourite nights out.

MALCOLM: Yes it is. He's your brother.

LUKE: [*motioning to the present*] I had other plans.

MALCOLM: She can wait. Agreed?

Pause.

LUKE: Sure.

MALCOLM: When you're trying to outstare death, Luke, things become clear-cut in a way that you can never imagine. My molecules, my genes are inside you, twined up like strands of rope. You are a part of me, Luke. You can't cut off any limb and get rid of me. Your atoms are mine, too. There is no God, Luke. When I die I can only escape nothingness through you. A part of me will live on in you and your brothers. You will be my connection to life. I am a ghost inside you, haunting you just as you will haunt your children.

◆ ◆ ◆ ◆ ◆

SCENE ELEVEN

Esther's living room. Late afternoon. ESTHER *is unwrapping a present. It is a beautiful green dress. She reads the card that has come with it.*

ESTHER: 'My dearest girl, I want to see you in it when we meet tomorrow. It will make undressing you even more exciting. Love, love, love, Luke.' Luke…

> *She ponders something for a moment, then reaches for her mobile phone and punches out a number.*

> [*Into the phone*] Luke? You must be getting ready for your bucks' night. Thank you for the dress, it's beautiful. Truly beautiful. I… Look, you've defeated me. I'm thinking of giving up my opposition to the project. You've got me. I love you, I love you. Have a wonderful night and stay away from the lap dancers—that's my job.

> *The doorbell rings.*

> Must go, my darling boy. 'Bye.

> ESTHER *exits and returns with* RAY.

> So what is it about the Hesperus Park project that's so urgent?

> RAY *looks around the room.*

RAY: What are you doing here?
ESTHER: What?
RAY: What are you doing here?
ESTHER: This is my house. What are you on about?
RAY: I've come to see you about a problem.
ESTHER: What problem?
RAY: You.

> *Pause.*

ESTHER: Who are you?

RAY: [*feeling the green dress*] Nice material. Nice colour.

ESTHER: What's this information you've got?

RAY: [*looking her up and down*] Nice legs. Nice breasts.

ESTHER: Please, I would like you to go.

RAY: The decision as to whether I go or not is mine alone.

ESTHER: Out.

> RAY *blows his nose.*

RAY: Don't you hate it when you can't get rid of a wog? My brain feels like a bowl of old custard. [*Pause.*] You're much better looking in the flesh. I can see what he sees in you. Actually I can see what both father and son saw in you. Do you think they compared notes about how good you are in the sack?

ESTHER: What in the hell are you talking about? Leave. Now!

RAY: My goodness you are firm, aren't you? I like a firm woman.

ESTHER: I'm going to call the police.

RAY: Esther? [*Pause.*] I wouldn't do that if I were you. I sometimes have a temper. [*Pause.*] I am under a considerable amount of pressure to find a quick solution. And you're the solution, Esther.

◆ ◆ ◆ ◆ ◆

SCENE TWELVE

Luke's driveway. Night. A happy LUKE *comes outside to go to his car, at the same time he's talking on his mobile phone.*

LUKE: No, sorry I'm late. I'm just going to hop into my car now. What's it called? Todd, you don't think a pole dancing place is a tad too clichéd for a bucks' night? I'll be there in about twenty minutes...

> *As he's talking, a car drives up. It stops, its headlights shining directly at* LUKE. *The sound of someone getting out of the car and its door slamming. The headlights are still on, so* LUKE *shields his eyes from the glare as a silhouetted figure comes towards him.* LUKE *steps out of the glare, so he can see who it is.*

Victor, is that you? What are you doing here?

VICTOR: I was hoping to catch you, Luke. Stand over there.

LUKE: What?

VICTOR: Stand over there, so I can see your lips.

> LUKE *does so and shields his eyes from the glare.*

LUKE: Look, I don't have much time, Victor. I'm on my way to my brother's bucks' night.

VICTOR: What night?

LUKE: Bucks' night.

VICTOR: Move further over. Into the light, I said.

> LUKE *does so.*

LUKE: What's up, Victor? You don't look happy. One of Ray's parrots die?

VICTOR: Ray doesn't know I'm here. I like you, Luke. Something's happened and I think you should know.

LUKE: Know what?

VICTOR: There's been a terrible accident.

◆ ◆ ◆ ◆ ◆

SCENE THIRTEEN

Hospital garden. Day. RAY *is sitting in a wheelchair. He is wearing an oxygen mask, with a canister of oxygen at his side. He takes a sniff of the oxygen.* VICTOR *enters.*

RAY: Where have you been, Victor? Where have you been?

VICTOR: I'm on time as usual.

RAY: Well, get here before time. I can't stand being around ill people, you know that.

VICTOR: Here in the sun, Ray. This is a nice spot.

> VICTOR *pushes* RAY *into the sun.* RAY *says something, but realises* VICTOR *can't understand because of the mask, which he takes off.*

RAY: It's good to be out of that damn room. I can breathe out here.

VICTOR: It's like an oasis.

RAY: What's that woman over there saying to that fellow, Victor?

VICTOR: That sick fellow?

RAY: They're sick, Victor! It's a hospital! Yeah, what's she so cut-up about.

Pause.

VICTOR: They're in Europe.

RAY: Who's in Europe?

VICTOR *continues to 'translate'.*

VICTOR: 'I've told them you haven't got much more time. They're cancelling the rest of their holiday and flying back.'

RAY: They'll be too late. He's a goner. Why am I surrounded by cadavers? This is a garden, why can't they all be back in their rooms? I come outside for some fresh air and sun and what do I find? A morgue.

LUKE *enters, wearing a tuxedo.*

Ah, here's our boy!

LUKE *stands before* RAY, *staring at him for a time.*

LUKE: You look as flash as a rat with a gold tooth, Ray.

RAY: A gold tooth would be quite good right now, dear boy. What's with the penguin suit?

LUKE: My brother's getting married today. I'm on my way to the church.

RAY: Pass on my apologies, but I won't be able to make it.

LUKE: You weren't invited. [*Pause.*] How do you feel?

RAY: Wretched. Fever. Sore throat. Muscle aches. Can't breathe properly.

LUKE: That's a pity.

VICTOR: I told him about those birds... they carry diseases.

RAY: Avian flu, Luke.

VICTOR: He got pneumonia from them. Dirty things.

RAY: The signs are not good.

LUKE: So you could die, Ray?

RAY: Typical of me to get a rare disease. I am entering the lag end of my life, I fear.

LUKE: One can only hope.

Pause.

RAY: You misled me, Luke.

LUKE: I misled you?

RAY: You said you would turn her. You said you could make Esther change her mind. Not much of the ladies' man, were you?

LUKE: How dare you. I loved her, Ray.

RAY: Love, love, love. Goodness me, sounds like a pop song.

LUKE: How did it happen, Ray?

RAY: The deed? She made a mistake. That's all.

LUKE: I want to know how she died.

RAY: That's too much information.

LUKE: How did she die?

RAY: You got my money? I rang your dad and he said you were bringing it. Got a lot of creditors after me. They are damn persistent. The good thing is that I can now throw them a few shekels and buy some time. I feel a winning streak coming on, Victor.

LUKE: How did Esther die?

RAY: Secret Ray's business.

LUKE: I will come at you so hard, Ray…

RAY: You're threatening me?

LUKE: Yes, I am.

RAY: Well, damn me, Luke, that was her problem. You know me, I wanted a calm conversation, one in which I would change her mind. I'm quite good at persuasion as you know, dear boy. She started to scream and yell, telling me to get out of her house and, you know, I wasn't feeling that well, this flu made me more jittery than usual. Then she hit me, telling me to leave. Well, you know, I don't like being hit, so I automatically hit her back and, gee, things got out of hand.

Pause.

LUKE: You killed her?

RAY: It got to such a stage that she was very sick… her head hit a table. I looked down, she was a bit of a mess and not breathing. That wasn't my intention, let me assure you of that. Then I thought, problem solved. Well, almost. I played with the electric wiring… you know me, I'm practically a pyromaniac.

LUKE: Then you set fire to the house.

RAY: It solved all our problems. The impediment to the project was gone and the police think she died in a house fire due to faulty wiring. No evidence. We're clear. You're clear. Your dad. Me. Victor.

LUKE: Did she feel pain? Did she know she was burning?

RAY: Keep your voice down. No. I told you she was dead.

Pause.

LUKE: I thought you were evil but you're just stupid.

RAY: No one says that to Raymond. [*Pause.*] It had to be done.

LUKE: Done? She left a message saying she was giving up! Didn't you ask her—?

RAY: She mentioned something like that—but that was only because she was under some pressure.

LUKE: She was going to give up.

RAY: You mean, I should have believed her?

LUKE: Are you thick?

Pause.

RAY: You're the thick one, Luke. Tell him, Victor. Tell him why he's thick. Tell him why he is a babe in the woods.

VICTOR: Esther was your father's mistress.

LUKE *smiles, believing* VICTOR *is joking.*

RAY: For about a decade, I believe. Not such a clever boy, are you? She didn't tell you, of course. Women like to keep those sort of secrets. They lie more than men believe.

LUKE: [*to* VICTOR] This is true?

RAY: Yeah, they are proficient liars.

VICTOR: That was why she tried to stop the development. It was her revenge on your father.

RAY: So put yourself in my shoes, Luke. If she could lie to you like that, then why was I going to believe her about stopping her opposition? People lie to save their lives, it's an extremely common reaction.

Pause.

LUKE: You both knew—from the beginning.

RAY: I thought it was interesting—son joying his father's mistress. There's a lot of frisson there—I mean from my point of view. I didn't know you were going to become keen on her. Gee, why would you go for a woman of that age? She had a nice body, though.

LUKE: You set me up—like some sort of a game?

RAY: You did think you were so smart, Luke. But you really didn't know anything. You see, that's what I was trying to teach you. I was going to tell you after you changed her mind. But you weren't quick or clever enough so I had to do your dirty business. That's okay, that's my job.

LUKE: You betrayed me.

RAY: *Au contraire,* I was trying to teach you the ways of the world.

LUKE: You don't understand, she meant everything to me.

RAY: Those sort of feelings pass—I'm a man of the world, I know these things.

LUKE: Did my father know?

RAY: Just recently.

LUKE: You told him?

>   RAY *looks to* VICTOR *to reply.*

VICTOR: He had to. Your father kept on asking why things were taking so long with Esther.

RAY: Look, Luke, when you get down to it, human beings are just strangely-shaped pieces of meat.

LUKE: No, we're not, Ray.

RAY: Get to my age and it's an inescapable fact of life.

>   *Silence.* LUKE *turns to* VICTOR *and mouths something.*

What are you on about? Victor, Victor, what's he on about?

VICTOR: You're not getting the money, Ray.

RAY: I fulfilled my part of the bargain.

LUKE: I had nothing to do with it, Ray. It was you.

RAY: You Boyces are all tied up in this. All of you are stained by this, like I am.

LUKE: How? There's no proof.

RAY: I want the money. Give me the money.

LUKE: The money's back in my safe.

RAY: Victor!

LUKE: Victor, you implicate me or my father and you'll end up in gaol, too. I want you to die in pain, Ray. I want you to die in poverty.

RAY: I'm going to bounce back and I'm going to come so hard at you.

LUKE: No, you won't, Ray. He isn't long for this world, is he, Victor?

>   *A resigned* VICTOR *shakes his head.*

RAY: You can't do this... it was a deal. I'll take all the Boyces with me.

LUKE: No, you won't, Ray. This is the end of the line for you.

Pause.

RAY: You knew nothing and you still know nothing.

LUKE: Oh, I do... I know I hate you, with a hate so deep that I want you to linger as long as possible. I want you to die in the deepest pain. I know you fear death, Ray. I want you to take a long time dying. I want you shit-scared of what is going to happen to you. Goodbye, Victor.

LUKE *goes. Silence.*

RAY: We're broke, Victor. Cold-stone broke. My mind is cramped. I'm at a loss. We will eat air. Get me out of here. I want to die in front of my birds.

VICTOR: We're damaged goods, Ray. Damaged goods.

RAY *puts on his oxygen mask as* VICTOR *wheels him off.*

SCENE FOURTEEN

The gardens of the Boyce mansion. MALCOLM *sits in a deckchair. He wears a tuxedo and sips a whisky. His thoughts are broken when* ESTHER, *wearing the green dress, comes and sits down on a piece of garden furniture. He glances at her and then away.*

MALCOLM: I can feel you, Esther. I can feel your hate.

Pause.

ESTHER: I won't close your eyes when you die, Malcolm. I want you to see death. I want you to see it.

MALCOLM: I'll see it soon enough. Don't be impatient, Esther.

LUKE *enters.*

You weren't at the church.

LUKE: I spent longer at the hospital than I thought.

MALCOLM: How is he?

LUKE: Very sick.

MALCOLM: What's the problem?

Danny Adock as Malcolm in the 2005 Griffin Theatre Company production of THE MARVELLOUS BOY. (Photo: Robert McFarlane)

LUKE: Got pneumonia from his birds.

MALCOLM: Nothing noble about that, is there? Did you give him the money?

LUKE: No.

MALCOLM: Why not?

LUKE: Because I decided not to. He's too sick to do anything to us.

MALCOLM: He might recover.

LUKE: Even if he does, he won't. There is no way we can be connected to Ray.

MALCOLM: Good boy. We'll need that cash. Looks lovely, doesn't it? Marquee... the flowers. You don't look so good, are you okay to make the speech?

LUKE: When did you know?

MALCOLM: About what?

LUKE: That I was seeing Esther.

MALCOLM: There's no need to go into that. It's over.

LUKE: When did you know?

MALCOLM: A few days ago.

LUKE: Ray tell you?

MALCOLM: I think he did.

LUKE: What did you feel?

MALCOLM: I felt... I felt she was using you.

LUKE: You weren't jealous?

MALCOLM: That would be petty. There's a bigger thing going on.

LUKE: Imagine my surprise when Ray told me. I was sort of an idiot boy in all of this, wasn't I?

MALCOLM: She was a clever woman. Attractive. Sometimes men don't think clearly when they're involved with a woman.

   Pause.

LUKE: You will have to tell me the truth on this. Did you tell Ray to hurt her? To kill her?

MALCOLM: No. No, that's wrong.

LUKE: Did you tell Ray to hurt her?

MALCOLM: When I found out what was happening, I told him he had to take control. He had to convince her to drop her opposition.

LUKE: Convince her! You know what that means to Ray.

MALCOLM: To scare her a little, yes, maybe—

LUKE: He was going to hurt her!

MALCOLM: I had no idea how he was going to do it.

LUKE: She was once your lover!

MALCOLM: She was a mad woman. All this has occurred because some woman decided to revenge herself on me because I walked out on her. She was out to get me. She wouldn't have cared if she dragged all of us down in bankruptcy.

LUKE: So you don't care that she's dead?

Pause.

MALCOLM: I wish it hadn't happened that way. But there it is. The road is clear now.

LUKE: Don't you feel anything for her?

MALCOLM: She lost any, any sympathy from me when she went after us in public. Not only me, all of us. Listen, remember what I said— you have to get your hands dirty... To go ahead in this business you have to do dubious things.

LUKE: Dubious things. Esther's dead!

Pause.

MALCOLM: I'm sorry it happened. I was annoyed with Ray for not telling me sooner that you were having a fling with her—

LUKE: Fling? Dad, I loved her.

MALCOLM: Come on, Luke—

LUKE: The words 'I loved her' aren't strong enough. The last thing I have of hers is a message she left on my phone. She tells me that she loves me. I listen to it all the time. I hear her voice and it is as if she is still alive, and yet I become scared because that's all I have of her: her voice. This morning I found a strand of her hair on my jacket. I kept it, like it was something magical, as if my mind could create her from it, like scientists creating something living from a strand of DNA. I am frightened to the core of my being that I will forget her, so I am deliberately recalling every moment we had together. The smell of her perfume, it is still there with the smell of her breath, her cunt. The tingle as her hair washes across my face. The moment she is at the kitchen door and turns back to smile at me. The frown of concentration as she reads a book, the moment her nipples became erect as I touch them, the softness of her belly, and I hear her laugh from another room—all these moments I am consciously calling up from inside me. Because I want to join them all together and make them firm in my mind so I don't forget her. Because if I forget her, I'm lost. No one, no one can ever warn you or explain to you how empty you feel when someone you love dies. When they're snatched from you. It's terrifying. Because there are moments when I think I'm waking from a nightmare and I think she's still alive and then it's like I'm suddenly drowning in this darkness, this emptiness. I have to remember her, remember every single thing or else there is nothing.

> *Pause.*

MALCOLM: My God, you did love her.

LUKE: What have you done to me? In all my life she was the one thing I've truly believed in.

> *Pause.*

MALCOLM: Time will be kind to you.

LUKE: I don't want it to. [*Pause.*] Did you love her?

> *Pause.*

MALCOLM: I was infatuated in the beginning… I liked her. Very much. But she took it much more seriously than I did. As it turned out.

LUKE: Then you don't know what it's like.

> *Pause.*

MALCOLM: All this is our secret.

LUKE: If you're a part of me then get out. Get out! You're a virus inside of me. Get out!

MALCOLM: Luke…

LUKE: I said, get out of me!

MALCOLM: Do you want to kill me, son? That's what I tried to do to *my* dad. He was always drunk, always beating up my mother. We ended up living in a garage. Yes, a fucking garage. It was lit by kerosene lamps and in winter, let me tell you, it chilled you to the bone. I'd have to go up to the local pub and plead with him to give me and my mum some money for food. One day, Luke, when I was thirteen, I decided that I was never going to live in poverty, I was never going to allow him to degrade us like he did. So as he slept I took to him with a piece of wood. Oh boy, did I make a mess of him. He lived. My mum and I took off. Never saw him again. All my life I have been consumed by a fury never to be poor, to work hard, to achieve. That woman wanted to bring me to my knees. She wanted me back in my father's cesspool. No one has done that to me—ever since the day I took to my father. [*Pause.*] I can't bring her back.

LUKE: [*motioning to his head*] She is in here. And I will not forget her or what you did to her. In destroying Esther, you destroyed me.

Pause.

MALCOLM: The guests are arriving. [*He stands.*] The project will start tomorrow. [*Pause.*] For your mother's sake, make a pleasant speech.

He exits. Silence.

LUKE: [*to himself*] Esther…

He falls to the ground and has a brief epileptic fit. ESTHER *turns away and then, as if remembering* LUKE*'s words to watch him when he has a fit, she turns back and looks.* LUKE *opens his eyes and realises what has happened, but he is too exhausted to care. He lies on the ground staring into the inner distance as the ghost of* ESTHER *stares at him.*

ESTHER: Luke…

Pause.

LUKE: Esther…

THE END

THE EMPEROR OF SYDNEY

Toby Schmitz as Luke in the 2006 Griffin Theatre Company production of THE EMPEROR OF SYDNEY. *(Photo: Robert McFarlane)*

FIRST PRODUCTION

The Emperor of Sydney was first produced by Griffin Theatre Company at the SBW Stables, Sydney, on 16 August 2006 with the following cast:

LUKE	Toby Schmitz
GILLIAN	Sibylla Budd
KEITH	Jack Finsterer
TODD	Alex Dimitriades
DIANE	Anita Hegh

Director, David Berthold
Designer, Nicholas Dare
Lighting Designer, Matthew Marshall

CHARACTERS

LUKE BOYCE
TODD BOYCE
KEITH BOYCE
GILLIAN
DIANE

SETTING

The Beauchamp mansion. The enormous living room. Night.
Time: now.

AUTHOR'S NOTE

The three sons are each possessed, in turn, by their dying father's
voice. This is indicated in the playscript by VOICE, followed by the
son's name who is channelling their father's voice at that point.
When the sons are 'possessed' by the voice, they remain on stage.
At no point do the other characters hear the possessed character
speak.

*The Beauchamp mansion. The enormous living room. Night. Malcolm
Boyce's dying, delirious voice emerges from the darkness as the lights
come on in the windows of a model of an upmarket apartment complex.
As we will see, the three sons are 'possessed' by their dying father's
voice.*

LUKE *enters, carrying a glass of whisky. He stops on seeing the lit-up
model.*

VOICE: [LUKE] We go to soil... become night soil... born in night
soil... things grow in soil. Buds. Seeds. Buildings grow... in soil...
Buildings grow in soil. Not air—in soil. The earth gives, the earth
takes away. We're bags of soil. We grow like night... nighty night...
nighty night...

> *He switches on the main light of the living room. Then he goes
> to the model and searches for its switch, which he turns off.
> Bemused, he examines the model.*

Kerosene lanterns smell, electricity doesn't. We are electricity. We
are earthed. We are earth. See, see the soil in my hand... Buildings
grow from my hand... A handful of soil is a handful of seeds.
Buildings grow at night, in night soil... Inherit the earth...

LUKE: [*to himself*] Just die, you fucker.

VOICE: [LUKE] Yes, see my handful of soil. I grow from it. You grow
from it... Buildings grow from it.

> LUKE *looks up at the ceiling as if he can see his father fall silent.*
> GILLIAN *enters.*

GILLIAN: What are you doing here, you fuck?

LUKE: Hello, Gillian.

GILLIAN: You're finally here.

LUKE: No, I'm the evil twin. Good Luke is arriving later.

GILLIAN: Your mum wanted you here yesterday.

LUKE: Only got back last night.

GILLIAN: But he could have died last night.

LUKE: But he didn't—did he?

GILLIAN: Why don't you go up and see him? Your mum's up there.

LUKE: I spoke to her on the phone this morning. She said he was much worse.

GILLIAN: It's very close, but he's fighting.

LUKE: What round?

GILLIAN: The nurse says she's never seen a man so determined to live.

LUKE: She's paid by the hour, so she's hoping he'll kick on. How's Mum?

GILLIAN: Drifting in and out of sleep.

LUKE: So would I if I had to listen to his ravings.

GILLIAN: They're not ravings.

LUKE: She said they were. Why, do they make sense to you?

GILLIAN: If you listen carefully. [*Pause.*] Why don't you go up there?

LUKE: [*re the model*] This thing has a mind of its own.

GILLIAN: What do you mean?

LUKE: Must be a faulty connection. How long do *you* think he has?

GILLIAN: The nurse says it's up to the patient.

LUKE: Is she being paid for her clichés? The idea is that when life is finished with you, you finish with life. I think he's forgotten that arrangement. I wish he'd gone to a hospice, instead of wanting to die at home. He's never been considerate of other's feelings.

> *Pause.*

GILLIAN: Are you trying to upset me?

LUKE: Why should I? He's not your father.

GILLIAN: He's my father-in-law, that makes it special.

LUKE: Special? In what way?

GILLIAN: Family.

LUKE: You hate my brother. Therefore you hate our family.

GILLIAN: I don't hate Keith. He annoys me sometimes.

LUKE: Shouting to your husband at parties: 'I wish you were dead!' Is that a term of endearment?

> *Pause.*

GILLIAN: I like your family for all its faults—and you're faulty.

LUKE: No, the wiring for this [*the model*] is faulty. Why don't you go back up there and watch the Great Fault die?

GILLIAN: Not enough room… There's your mum… Diane. Diane's made it her duty.

LUKE: [*sardonically*] Oh, she's a queer one, that Diane, isn't she? One moment a stranger, the next she's bending the ear of Dad out of shape.

GILLIAN: Hey, a drink thank you.

LUKE: Keith said that you'd stopped.

GILLIAN: A man is dying above my head... surely that's a good excuse for a drink.

LUKE: Same?

GILLIAN: Anything you drink, Luke, is fine by me. How was your vacation?

LUKE: Venice is a bit like Dad—it's in its death throes but refuses to die. Gee, Gillian, don't you feel his weight pushing down on us? Why can't he die in the basement?

GILLIAN: He had a tough childhood, Luke. He had his own awful dad. He suffered too.

LUKE: Suffering does not make people kind, it makes them hard.

As he pours her a drink, GILLIAN *examines the model.*

GILLIAN: Is this to scale?

LUKE: Apparently.

GILLIAN: You know, I met this famous architect once. What's his name? Real old. Who cares? He looked like a used condom. I'd been in a couple of his apartments and they were really expensive. But the thing was that the ceilings were really low and I wondered if he did that to save money... But, you see, he was really short, like a dwarf, so he built everything for men his height. What an ego he had. Aggressive too, like all short men.

LUKE: [*giving her the drink*] This architect is rather tall.

GILLIAN: [*tasting the drink*] Ah, that's the end of the longest three days of my life. [*Looking intently at the model*] It looks like a doll's house. I had a doll's house, did you?

LUKE: No, my mother probably thought it would play havoc with my sexual orientation.

GILLIAN: This project is costing a fortune, isn't it?

LUKE: You don't know how much it has cost already, Gillian.

As GILLIAN *fiddles with a switch a small sign lights up: 'The Boyce'.*

GILLIAN: Hey, did you see this sign—The Boyce?

LUKE: Maybe they should have added a big grinning face on the front.

GILLIAN: I thought it was called Hesperus Park?

LUKE: The ogre above, pushing down on our heads, wants it called after our family.

GILLIAN: I love the name Hesperus. Female, you see. Vesper, the evening star. Venus. Hesperus. But you knew that?

LUKE: 'Fraid not. Didn't Keith tell you about the new name?

GILLIAN: He never tells me anything.

KEITH *enters wearing a tuxedo.*

KEITH: Maybe because you don't listen.

GILLIAN: What did you say?

KEITH: [*noticing the model*] What's that doing here?

LUKE: It was here when I arrived.

KEITH: It should be back in the showroom. [*Noticing the sign*] What's with the sign?

GILLIAN: I thought you'd know.

KEITH: First time I've seen it. If that's in proportion, it's going to be a fucking big sign on the real thing.

LUKE *has noticed that* KEITH *is wearing a tuxedo and that* GILLIAN *is also dressed up.*

LUKE: Why are you two dressed up? Isn't it a little early to celebrate?

KEITH: Got a message from Mum while we were at the opera, telling us Dad had taken a turn for the worse. The good thing was that we didn't have to sit through the last five hours of *Götterdämmerung*.

LUKE: Well, you know how it ends, don't you?

KEITH: Don't spoil it, just in case I have to sit through the whole thing one day. How is the old man, now?

LUKE: Close to the end apparently.

GILLIAN: Where have you been?

KEITH: Ablutions. Has he been asking for me?

LUKE: I thought he was out of it?

KEITH: For brief moments he seems lucid, the rest of the time it's loony tunes and gibberish.

GILLIAN: It's not gibberish, you don't listen carefully enough.

KEITH: [*motioning to her whisky*] I thought you were—

GILLIAN: No willpower I'm afraid.

KEITH: That's a surprise. But then, you did lay off the drink for three days. [*To* LUKE] Mum?

LUKE: Haven't been up there yet. I imagine she's sitting by his side. Adoration. Tears. Forgiveness. Wasted on him, really.

KEITH: I'll have a look in. It's cold in here.

GILLIAN: Your dad says he's too hot. He wants the airconditioner on.

KEITH: Upstairs maybe, but not down here.

GILLIAN: There's something wrong with the airconditioning—it either works for the whole house or not at all.

LUKE: I've always thought hell should be cold.

GILLIAN: Let's hope this project doesn't have the same airconditioning firm.

KEITH: [*to* GILLIAN] Try and moderate... What the fuck! Drink as much as you like. You see, Luke, she wants me to be the handbrake in the marriage; that way she can bitch about me. But she can't, can you?

GILLIAN *salutes* KEITH *with her glass as he exits.*

GILLIAN: [*to* LUKE] Why are you sarcastic about your mother's tears and forgiveness? Death is the great reckoning and it's a time of forgiveness. Children also have an obligation to forgive their parents at this time.

LUKE: That's a very banal thing to say, Gillian. I expected something sharper than that.

GILLIAN: Your father is a part of you.

LUKE: [*pretending to pluck at himself to get 'rid' of father*] Get out. Get out of me!

GILLIAN: So he is you?

LUKE: Children are merely genetic parodies of their parents. You forgive your mother when she died?

GILLIAN: My biggest regret in life is that I didn't make friends with my mother. The day before she died, she was in bed. She played with my hair and suddenly said, 'When you were little you were auburn, auburn, auburn, and now you're blonde'. I could see such love in her eyes. And I thought, 'God, why could we never be friends?' It was like a war between us. I forgave her, she didn't forgive me. Your father obviously hurt you. [*Pause.*] You don't want to talk about it, do you?

LUKE: Women talk a problem to death, men just kill it.

TODD *enters, carrying an old plastic children's bucket.*

TODD: Luke, I didn't expect you.

LUKE: Heard his death rattle. Hey, isn't that my old bucket?

TODD: Found it under the stairs.

LUKE: You giving it to your bub? I might want to keep it.

GILLIAN: [*noticing something in it*] What's that?

TODD: Soil. I went to the site and got some soil.

GILLIAN: Hesperus Park?

TODD: Boyce Park. I thought he would like it. It's confirmation. Confirmation that the project's started.

LUKE: What's he going to do—eat it?

TODD: Your time away didn't do you any good. [*To* GILLIAN] How's things upstairs?

GILLIAN: Same, I think.

> KEITH *enters.*

That was quick.

KEITH: Just poked my head in the door.

GILLIAN: How is he?

KEITH: Dozing, then waking up, yelling, talking, not making sense. [*To* LUKE] I told Mum you were down here. I'm going to get her a cup of tea.

TODD: [*re the bucket*] I'll take this up.

KEITH: Diane said you'd gone to the site to get some soil. That's it?

TODD: Yes.

LUKE: We can sprinkle it on his coffin.

TODD: We will.

KEITH: Is this your idea or Diane's?

> *An irritated* TODD *begins to exit.*

LUKE: Hey, Toddie.

TODD: It's Todd.

LUKE: Well, Todd. Did you put this miniature feat of sign engineering on the model? The Boyce.

TODD: Why not? It's called The Boyce. Last night we brought him down and showed him. He cried. [*He switches off the sign.*] Anything else?

LUKE: Maybe he cried because the name was spelt wrongly—you know how you were always bad at spelling.

KEITH *and* LUKE *laugh.*

KEITH: Why didn't you just get some soil from outside, he wouldn't have known the difference.

TODD: Actually he would have. You two wouldn't know the difference.

TODD *exits.*

KEITH: [*to* LUKE] What's with him?

GILLIAN: You two always put him down.

LUKE: You know what people used to say about him when he was a kid? Keith reads the comics and Todd looks at the pictures.

GILLIAN: What about you?

LUKE: I wrote them.

GILLIAN: I don't think your holiday was long enough. I'll get the tea for your mum.

GILLIAN *exits.*

KEITH: It means she can secretly top up her glass in the kitchen. [*Pause.*] One moment Dad thinks Todd's the prodigal son… the next… He took one look at the grandson and it's like all is forgiven, forgotten. You don't think Todd and Diane were a bit obvious naming it after Dad. I suspect the hand of Diane in that.

LUKE: You're a suspicious thing, Keith.

KEITH: You haven't been here while the old man is dying. Diane dotes over him. Talks to him, whispers sweet nothings in his ear, combs his hair, manicures his fingernails. She only married into the family— what is it?—four months ago. Remember the wedding reception? She spent most of her time dancing with Dad, not Todd. Maybe it was to get away from her father. What a speech. The hick probably thought it was a stag night down at the footy club. [*Motioning to the model*] What do you think of it?

LUKE: You'd have to be pretty tiny to live in there.

KEITH: Dad always wanted to build something upmarket.

LUKE: How long before it's finished?

KEITH: They're keeping to schedule.

KEITH *goes to examine the model.*

VOICE: [LUKE]: Why would she let herself go like that? Pissing herself... Jeez... That fucking foreman will have to go. A hard nut, a hard nut like Ray will handle him. Lean on him a little, Ray. Lean of those fellas I point out to you. Have a quiet word in their ears. A hard word.

KEITH *switches the sign on and off and laughs.*

LUKE: What's so funny?

KEITH: He cried looking at this fucking thing. Hit him with a sledge-hammer and he wouldn't blink. Show him a kid's toy and he cries. You ever see him cry?

LUKE: Too horrible to contemplate.

KEITH: But Todd gets to see him cry.

Pause.

LUKE: What's your point?

KEITH: No point, yet. Better see if Gillian had made the tea. The mysteries of boiling water have always escaped her.

KEITH *exits.*

VOICE: [LUKE] You laugh... you laugh at me, but let me tell you, buster, I'll have the last laugh. My firm will destroy yours. You will learn to hate my name because it will be everywhere. My genes are my name. My name is carved into your brain. Seared into it. Grilled into it. My will is stronger than yours, buster. Buster Keaton, a wall fell on him and he lived to tell the tale. Walls fall on me and I live to tell the tale.

DIANE *enters and silently watches* LUKE *turn the sign off and on several times. She laughs. Then he notices her.*

DIANE: You like it?

LUKE: Small things amuse small minds. You seem to be bearing up well, Diane. Dad been playing with his soil?

DIANE: He knows what it is and what it means.

LUKE: What does it mean?

DIANE: The Boyce is on its way. Your father is so pleased with the response to it. The media says it's all in good taste.

LUKE: Good taste is when vulgarity becomes the norm.

Pause.

DIANE: Why don't you go up and see him?

LUKE: I'm not in the right frame of mine right now.

DIANE: Your mother wants you up there.

Pause.

LUKE: The sign your idea?

DIANE: Todd's.

LUKE: How's Malcolm?

DIANE: What? What are you on about?—he's dying.

LUKE: Your son. You know, his namesake.

DIANE: At our place, with the nanny. Just in case tonight... Your father loves him.

LUKE: If I had a grandchild named after me, I would too.

DIANE: He loves him because he is also his only grandchild. He said Malcolm was his future. You and Keith haven't given your father a future like that.

LUKE: The future is the last thing I'd want to give him.

Pause.

DIANE: How was Venice?

LUKE: Same as usual. Gondolas filled with overweight English women escaping from a failed love affair pretending to be jolly.

DIANE: You're so lucky.

LUKE: Lucky?

DIANE: I've seen Venice in movies. It looks so beautiful. Todd said he'll take me there.

She looks around the room and smiles.

LUKE: Wipe that smile off your face... he's not dead yet... You'll have to temper your celebrations until he really does kick the bucket.

DIANE: It's this room. This house. I was here, not long before your father bought it. I used to be a babysitter for a wealthy family who lived in the next street. When I'd get off at the bus stop I'd walk past here and stare through the gates. The whole place was rundown, all the flower beds overgrown, the tennis court was covered with weeds. The family used to send me home in a taxi. One night as the taxi was passing here, I told the driver to stop and I got out. I don't know what possessed me, but I wanted to see inside this house. I crawled over the fence and broke a window and climbed in. It was dark and smelt of mould. Possums were in the roof and there were mice or rats—probably both. I went from room to room and I could feel the ghosts. I could hear them. In the ballroom I could hear music, laughing, talking. Everyone was dressed to the nines. The furniture—I could see the furniture of the era when it was the most magnificent mansion in the whole of Sydney. In the bedrooms I could see people sleeping, making love. I could hear the giggles of the housemaids as they ran down the hallways. I was possessed by the past in this house. I saw beyond the ruined rooms and rotten curtains into another world. And now, it's here. Now I am a part of it. I used to daydream I would be here one day and I am. I stood in this room, Luke, this very room. My mouth was open with wonder, even though it was a damp ruin. I was amazed at how big it was. Broken mirror on the wall there. Old couch. Peeling wallpaper. Frayed, stinking carpet. I looked around the room and imagined what it must have been once like it is now. Exactly. I am standing here, in this room, and it's real. Why are you smiling? You mocking me?

LUKE: I think it's a sweet story. Ever told Todd?

DIANE: No, it's a silly story. I thought you'd like a silly story. But there is one thing, Luke. That's why I admire your father. He bought this house and restored it to its former glory.

LUKE: Because it's the biggest mansion in Sydney. So people wouldn't look down on him for building cheap housing. He hates being considered nouveau riche, that's all.

DIANE: The point is—he bought it and restored it. He kept the ghosts alive. If you had half the…

LUKE: Half the what… Diane?

DIANE: You were born into wealth, I was born into poverty. You went to private schools, I went to public schools. My father is a truck driver. I know strength and purpose when I see it. And I admire it because I know what it's like to be at the mercy of someone who doesn't have it.

LUKE: Todd has it? Or is he living off your strength and power?

DIANE: You don't know your brother very well. The baby and your father's dying has changed him.

Pause.

LUKE: Maybe his dying will change me—we'll see, shall we?

DIANE: He's much changed since you last saw him. The cancer's eaten away his stomach. He has to sit up in bed. The pressure's less on his insides that way. He's in and out of consciousness. Sometimes he's talking about night soil, then it's Buster Keaton. Just before, I took his hands and said, 'I'm here'. He opened his eyes and didn't know who I was at first. Then he remembered and was very happy and so was I. I squeezed his hands too hard and he said I was hurting him. He said he had paid his debt.

LUKE: Death is a great debt collector. But, Diane, he can never pay off his debt. It's only because of my mother, you realise, that I'm going to do this.

VOICE: [LUKE] Mercy, mercy me. Save me, Malcolm. Save me from your father. On some enchanted evening, save me. I have been a good man. I have been a good man. I will come back and haunt you.

> LUKE *exits.* DIANE *spins around, smiling to herself, then she hears* KEITH *enter.*

KEITH: Strange to see you down here.

DIANE: Why strange?

KEITH: I thought you were welded to my father's bed.

> KEITH *goes to get himself a drink.*

DIANE: What do you mean by that?

KEITH: You happy he's dying?

> *She wonders what he's talking about.*

The little dance.

DIANE: As I told Luke: this room, this house makes me happy.

KEITH: Then you'll always be happy.

DIANE: You're cryptic.

KEITH: I think you understand me.

> *Pause.*

DIANE: Todd said the apartments are selling very well already.

KEITH: Yes.

DIANE: Then you must be in two minds about its success.

KEITH: How so?

DIANE: You were against the project, weren't you?

KEITH: We were financially drowning. This was an extravagance. A monument to my father's ego.

DIANE: It's an extravagance that worked.

KEITH: By the skin of our teeth, Diane. If that environmentalist hadn't died at the last moment we would have gone under. So despite your dreams of what Boyce will do next, I wouldn't think too extravagantly—it was a lucky gamble that paid off.

DIANE: I'm just pleased for you three brothers.

KEITH: That's nice to know.

> *Pause.*

DIANE: I know you don't like me.

KEITH: It's not that, it's just that I don't trust you.

DIANE: Why, what could I do to you?

KEITH: Nothing.

DIANE: Maybe you just don't like women. Maybe you mistrust all women. Maybe you equate Gillian with all women.

KEITH: She thinks her madness makes her interesting. You're interesting to me, Diane. You come into our lives by getting pregnant to Todd—

DIANE: You think it was deliberate? That I'd get knocked up in order to do what?

KEITH: Join our family.

> *Pause.*

DIANE: And you say your father has an ego. I met Todd and fell in love with him. Our baby. Your father. Your mother.

KEITH: But not me and Luke?

> *Pause.*

DIANE: Do you love me? [*Pause.*] Do you think Luke loves me? I remember you from the wedding reception. I walked out of the marquee and heard you sniggering and laughing about my father and mother to one of the waiters. 'The Hillbillies have landed,' you said. Quite loudly. [*Pause.*] Am I a hillbilly like my parents?

KEITH: You're too shrewd for that, Di.

DIANE: Diane. I'm not ashamed of them.

KEITH: Oh, yes you are, Princess Di. When your father was giving his speech and he'd get to another dirty joke, I would see you flush and your smile became as tight as a cat's arse. Your face beamed with hidden humiliation. Diane, Diane, you've made it. You're a Boyce, you're part of a dynasty, you're top of the world. I'll have a bet with you. You'll see your parents—maybe once a year: Christmas afternoons. Their place, not here. Do you love them as much as you love Todd, our mother, our father? Your shit stinks like everybody's. It stinks to high heaven like Dad's shit now stinks.

DIANE: Scatology becomes you.

KEITH: Do you want a drink or do you want to be perfectly sober so you can remember his death and your appropriate performance? Because you used to be an actress, didn't you? That is, before you called yourself an interior decorator.

DIANE: I did a course in interior design.

KEITH: Didn't finish.

DIANE: Got pregnant.

Pause.

KEITH: Were you any good as an actress?

DIANE: I had some good notices... you know, reviews.

KEITH: Yes, I do know. I looked you up on the net. Amazing what stuff percolates about someone through the eternity of cyberspace. If I were to make a judgement about your career as an actress—

DIANE: And you know so much about theatre—

KEITH: I would say that you were probably too intelligent to be an actor. I always think that great actors have to have a touch of stupidity. And judging by the reviews, that was your failing. You didn't have it... that—

DIANE: That *something*?

KEITH: I haven't read so many reviews that called an actor's performances 'intelligent'. What does that mean?

DIANE: That I wasn't sexy enough, actually.

KEITH: Summation—not stupid enough, not sexy enough?

DIANE: Yes. And I'm going to be perfectly honest with you, Keith—

KEITH: Honesty from someone who wanted to pretend to be other people.

Pause.

DIANE: To pretend to be someone else and get away with it is the greatest escape in the world. It means, Keith, that you're no longer living in

a fibro house in the middle of the sticks. Sticks is the wrong word.
The soil was too poor to grow sticks. Stuck in the middle of endless
paddocks, surrounded by fibro houses and losers and violence and
welfare mums and... well, you name it. In my head I could be a
queen, a scientist—attractive, of course, no one wants to be a plain
scientist—a model, a dying beauty dying for love. And then I'm
rudely awoken by my dad whacking my mother across the face
so hard her cheeks shatter. Who wouldn't want to pretend to be
somewhere else, someone else? Now, before you applaud my sob
story, allow me to let you into a little secret I learnt. Sometimes
someone from my background wants *it* too much. I was good,
Keith. Fucking good, but I lacked something—not stupidity—I
lacked the proper background. One of the most important things
I learned was that the actresses who make it are invariably from
comfortable backgrounds. You see, they've had those fucking acting
lessons since they were five. They've been told they're beautiful
from the moment they opened their eyes. If they truly suffered in
life they wouldn't be able to hide it. You need to have no suffering,
no hurt, just the belief that everything will come to you. And it does.
I carried too many thoughts, too many dreams in my head, and they
swirled around and everyone thought it was intelligence. It was in
fact hunger, a desperate hunger to be brilliant, to be adored. You've
got no idea how those reviews hurt me. I wanted to be vacuous.

KEITH *laughs, she smiles in return.*

I'm not making it up. I did. One time I was acting in a French farce
next to a cute young thing. Perfect face for films. I had to hand her an
address book that contained the telephone numbers of her husband's
girlfriends, which she didn't know about. She slowly turned page
after page as if she were reading fucking *War and Peace*. I mean,
the silence went on for minutes, it seemed. I would have glanced at
a couple of names and slammed the book with a cry of anguish. But
she took her time, because she knew the audience adored her and
would wait an eternity for her to finish reading the book. Finally
she closed the book and sighed, 'There are so many'. My heart sank
because I knew I didn't have the confidence to be able to do nothing
and believe I was going to be watched and adored by the audience
who would sigh when I sighed.

Pause.

KEITH: But I'm watching you now and I believe your performance. [*Pause.*] Are you performing now?

DIANE: You tell me.

She examines the model and feels it.

VOICE: [TODD] Lord, this is pain. Lordy Lord. Morphine, girlie. Nobody knows but me, nobody knows but me, O Lordy Lord. Your mother, Toddy, Todd, Todd, your mother would jump over the moon and fetch the cheese for you, you know what…? My hands are not soft. Most girls like it hard.

DIANE: I like this, it's beautiful. Do you like this, Keith? [*Pause.*] You think I'm a gold-digger.

KEITH: You tell me.

DIANE: Well, you'll have to make a decision on that, won't you?

TODD *enters quietly, not noticed by* KEITH *and* DIANE.

KEITH: But you'd like to be mistress of this house?

DIANE: Wouldn't anybody? I'd have that chandelier dusted more often.

KEITH: There's some cleaning rags in the kitchen pantry.

DIANE: You can't get rid of me, Keith. I'm family.

KEITH: How goes it upstairs, Todd?

DIANE: [*surprised*] Todd…

Pause.

TODD: It won't be long now. He woke up before. Then said, clear as a bell, 'Your mother is very good in sick rooms'. Then said his sap, his very soul was pouring out of him, like the piss. 'It's not my time,' then, 'Oh, yes, it is my time.'

DIANE: What about a priest?

TODD: Mum asked. He doesn't want a priest.

KEITH: [*quoting*] 'Priests are ghouls on your soul. They want your soul.' Is Luke there?

TODD: Bit creepy. He's just standing there, watching him. Not saying or doing anything.

KEITH: Luke's special, that's why he does things like that. [*To* DIANE] Nice sheer blue dress.

DIANE: What?

KEITH: Last Sunday's papers—society pages. Your tummy's so svelte now. You look after yourself well. And you, Todd, they called you scion of the Boyce family. We're all scions. You think Dad has ever heard of that word?

DIANE: He's brave. To stop chemotherapy so he could see this project through, knowing he had only a few months to live, that's brave. Does Luke really want him dead? [*Pause.*] What is it with this project? Why's he so bitter?

KEITH: *Cherchez la femme.*

TODD: There was this woman, Esther Tucker. She was very successful in opposing this project.

KEITH: Environmental reasons.

TODD: It was very personal. She spread lots of rumours about us. It was costing us a fortune. The interest rates were killing us. If the project stalled too long—

KEITH: We were going to go under.

TODD: I don't know the full story. Luke tried to convince her to drop her opposition. I mean, she was brilliant at using the media. Apparently she used to be a journalist, so she knew just how to get the right newsworthy slant.

DIANE: So Luke talked to her?

TODD: And talked. And talked. Keith and I didn't know about this. He kept it a secret.

KEITH: And then he fell for her.

DIANE: She must have been very attractive.

KEITH: She must have had something because she was much older than him.

DIANE: A fire… she died in a fire. Now, I remember. It was in the papers.

KEITH: She died in a house fire. There were rumours that it could have been foul play, that someone killed her and set fire to the house. The coincidence was far too great—the Boyces wanted to get rid of her and she died in a house fire. Very convenient for us.

DIANE: [*to* TODD] Did you know about this?

TODD: Much as Keith, I think.

DIANE: People think that Malcolm had something to do with it?

KEITH: Of course, for the general public nothing is beyond the Boyce family.

DIANE: Why would he do that?

TODD: She was the only thing from stopping it going ahead.

Pause.

DIANE: Did Malcolm know Luke was having an affair with her?

TODD *shrugs.*

KEITH: Who knows.

DIANE: Do you believe that someone killed her? She was your dad's enemy. He must have been relieved when she went.

TODD: He was sort of... depressed for a couple of days. There was no celebrating. Even though her death saved us.

DIANE: Why didn't you tell me this?

TODD: Why? It was just rumours. The police cleared Dad.

DIANE: But Luke believes that your father arranged for this woman to die?

TODD: Yes, he does. He's consumed by the idea.

KEITH: She must have meant a lot to him. I never thought Luke capable of grief.

DIANE: That's why he ran away to Venice?

KEITH: Venice? He was hardly there. I was having drinks with a merchant banker a few days ago. He had just done a deal in Holland. He ran into Luke in Amsterdam. He made no sense at all. Luke has spent the past two months in Amsterdam stoned and out of his gourd.

Pause.

DIANE: Poor Luke.

KEITH: Poor Luke... He's just milking it for all it's worth. I might go up there and make sure he doesn't try to kill the old man.

DIANE: [*as* KEITH *is about to exit*] Keith.

KEITH: Yes, Diane.

DIANE: If Luke is in such a bad way, what he's going to do in the company once... you know, once your father's gone?

KEITH: I don't think we really have to make a decision now, do we?

KEITH *exits.*

VOICE: [LUKE] I'm not fucking ready, pissant. I'll be back. I'm a molecule inside you, tiny as a flea. [*He belches.*] I've whipped four thousand fellows with this arm. Well, of course, they're not wogs,

if only they would work like wogs. Poor white trash whip the wogs.
Oh, when I was courting you—what dreams—I handed you my
dreams on a platter.

TODD: Sometimes... sometimes you're... eager. Too eager.

DIANE: What do you mean—eager? I'm ambitious for you. I don't
want to be dishonest. It's how I feel. Your brothers just don't know,
Todd, how important you've become to your father. How much he
has come to love you.

TODD: He loves you.

DIANE: But your brothers are jealous of that. Last night, when you were
on the site, I was alone with your father. He sat up and asked me
to sit next to him on a chair. He said, 'You're very beautiful. May
I do this to you?' And he reached out and put his hand up my dress
and felt my cunt and then said, 'You know, that's what life is about.
Nothing else.'

TODD: You allowed him to do that?

DIANE: There was no lechery involved.

TODD: His hand touching your cunt?

DIANE: He's a dying man. It represented life to him.

TODD: That's a novel take. I might try it on the women I meet. 'Excuse
me, there's no lechery involved, I just want to feel your cunt.'

DIANE: You're not jealous, are you?

TODD: Jealous? No. Appalled? Yes.

DIANE: It wasn't untoward. It was an old man realising what life is
about.

TODD: Your cunt?

DIANE: Well, yes. You see, when I first met him, I thought he had the
strongest life force of any man I have ever known. And even though
he is dying, he is still fighting the world. I like that. I like that male
force. That was his hand up my dress... he's saying that's what it's
all about—the life force. I liked what he did. Because I knew what
he was saying.

TODD: I'm a little behind in all of this. It's like the presents you give
him, without telling me.

DIANE: They're presents from the both of us. Remember, Todd, I
brought you and your father back together.

TODD: You being pregnant did. He was desperate for a grandson...
someone to pass the name on.

DIANE: I spent a lot of time singing your praises. And now... he sees you in a totally different light. He knows you won't let him down. He sees in us... continuity. He doesn't see that in Luke and Keith. [*Pause.*] You didn't tell me about Luke and that woman.

Pause.

TODD: There was the wedding... you being pregnant... Dad sick... Diane, I'm trying to balance a lot of things at the moment.

DIANE: What do you mean by that?

TODD: I wish you'd just tone down your—

DIANE: Jesus Christ, tone down what?

TODD: I am under a lot of pressure.

DIANE: We both are.

TODD: It is me, Diane. That is *my* father dying. There is what is happening now. And what will happen in the future. There's Mum. My brothers.

DIANE: What are you saying?

TODD: A man is dying—it's about him.

DIANE: It's not only about him. It's about everybody connected to him.

TODD: Just as a favour for me. I think sometimes your ambition can be misconstrued. Especially at a time like this.

Pause.

DIANE: Is ambition a bad thing? You're ambitious now. That's a good thing, isn't it? I'm out of the mire, Todd. If you only knew the humiliation I felt at our wedding. How embarrassing my father was—not only in his crude speech—but all day. And then at the end of the reception, I went looking for him before we left on our honeymoon, and he was vomiting in a flower bed. I couldn't even say goodbye to him. Because, really, I'd said it years before. I have escaped that world—I make no bones about that. Your father's ambition pushed through this project. He made it happen out of sheer will. As you will, Todd, because I believe in you. My whole being believes in you. Don't be gentle with me.

TODD: What do you mean?

DIANE: No one can break me. I am unbreakable. Fuck me as if you want to break me. I want that. I want you to become your father. Because we have this future together and we're going to do great things. Ambitious things. The Boyce name will be a byword.

TODD: A byword for what?

DIANE: Everything that's wonderful. Boyce Park is the start. Everything your father did has been just a lead-up to this new beginning. So don't be gentle with me. [*Pause.*] And don't be gentle with your brothers. They'll want to put you in your place.

GILLIAN *enters with an empty glass as* DIANE *kisses* TODD.

GILLIAN: Get a room! Ah, the good stuff's in here.

She pours herself a drink.

TODD: Luke still up there?

GILLIAN: No. But my husband has put in an appearance. God, that nurse is dreadful, isn't she? Just because she's ugly she thinks she's intelligent. Excuse me. Drink?

TODD: No.

DIANE: No.

GILLIAN: [*to* TODD] He was mentioning your name.

Pause.

Anita Hegh as Diane and Alex Dimitriades as Todd in the 2006 Griffin Theatre Company production of THE EMPEROR OF SYDNEY. *(Photo: Robert McFarlane)*

TODD: I'll pop up for a moment. [*To* DIANE] Call if you need me.

TODD *exits. An uncomfortable silence between the two women.*

GILLIAN: Words are used to overcome our fear of silence. So don't think you have to say anything.

Silence.

DIANE: It's awkward. Never been in this position before. Someone close dying close by. [*Pause.*] You don't like Todd?

GILLIAN: What makes you say that?

DIANE: You... you seem to make yourself distant from him.

GILLIAN: Does he complain about that?

DIANE: No, it's my observation.

GILLIAN: I'm not conscious I'm doing it. But in future I'll make a concerted effort to be more... friendly. It's my manner.

DIANE: I'm trying to figure something out...

GILLIAN: Goodness me, you've always struck me as someone who reaches conclusions without trying to figure anything out. [*Pause.*] Sorry... the emotions of the occasion. I'm not used to someone close by dying, either. Question?

DIANE: Todd. Why did his brothers and father treat him so badly?

GILLIAN: Hasn't Todd told you?

DIANE: He just says that they did.

GILLIAN: They did. Keith is sharp, a meticulous planner, a good card player. An anchor. Luke mixes well with people, has a good sense of architecture. He balances Malcolm's roughness. Todd didn't do well at school and felt he was overlooked. And if you feel that, it happens that you are overlooked. He could never relax into a role. He wanted to do well, don't get me wrong, but he would lose... concentration. That's it. He wanted to work, wanted to party, wanted to screw—all at the same time. But you must understand one thing, Diane. Once Malcolm senses a weakness in anybody, including a son, he smells it—the merest whiff of a weakness and he goes for you. So he'd pick on Todd and Todd didn't know how to come back at his father. As far as Malcolm was concerned Todd didn't have the nous for business, didn't have the people skills and couldn't even back it up with sporting prowess. But he had a good eye... good eyes for interior design. Poofter skills. Didn't... concentrate enough on it, though. I suppose he didn't have the confidence and Malcolm is very, very good at destroying someone's confidence.

DIANE: You don't know how tough Todd is underneath. This is his last chance. He knows that.

GILLIAN: You never know—maybe Todd will be set free by Malcolm's death. I have a soft spot for him. Everyone picks on someone in life. I went out with him a couple of times before I started to go out with Keith.

DIANE: You went out with Todd?

GILLIAN: Nightclubs. Restaurants.

DIANE: For how long?

GILLIAN: Couple of months.

DIANE: He didn't mention anything about it.

GILLIAN: Why should he?

DIANE: They're brothers.

GILLIAN: Sometimes I wonder if one of them is a changeling. [*Pause. Answering* DIANE*'s unspoken question*] Yes, we did. [*Pause.*] Hard to compare notes. Very different, those two brothers.

   Pause.

DIANE: Why did you break up?

GILLIAN: He was very messed-up. He complained about his lot in life… and I didn't want to listen to that. I didn't want to hear about anyone's demons. Or in his case—the demon. His father. I just wanted a good time. Then I married Keith. I should have cradled-snatched Luke. Trouble was that Luke was adored by everyone. Everyone loves the runt of the litter. And, boy, like some runts, he flourished by being adored and cared for. His dad, his mum… just loved him. Keith thinks he's frivolous—that's probably the strongest criticism I've ever heard from his lips. Whatever Luke turned his attention to, he would master it quick as a flash. It was as if Malcolm was as dazzled by Luke as other people were. So Todd was leapfrogged because Todd, well, he was a tortoise compared to Luke's rabbit. And the wonderful thing about Luke is that he could have any woman, because he's so nice, attentive, funny, but he never played the field. And because he seemed unattainable, women chased after him. Many a wet patch has been left on these chairs and couches by women wanting him. But, you see, he was so adored, he just got used to it. Like a plant that's used to sunlight—just takes it for granted. So there was no need to desire anything. And now he's hurt... and I have to say I'm pleased. I've waited years for him to be hurt.

DIANE: So you were keen on him, too?

GILLIAN: That's my wet patch there. [*A beat.*] Yeah, I know. I'm crude.

Pause.

DIANE: Are you having any children?

GILLIAN: I believe that sex is a prerequisite for conception. So Malcolm could end up with only one grandson. [*Pause.*] In a way these three brothers have helped ruin my life.

Pause.

DIANE: But you're well?

Pause.

GILLIAN: Do I look unwell?

DIANE: I just mean those hospital stays... the latest one helped?

GILLIAN: Nuthouse stays, actually. Why? Do I make you uneasy? Are you afraid of me? I might go... *crazy*!

DIANE: [*laughing*] No. No. I sometimes wonder how fragile that makes a person.

GILLIAN: Like a Fabergé egg?

Pause.

DIANE: It was a kind question. I was showing an interest in you. After all, I'm your sister-in-law.

GILLIAN: Well, Di, I'm a hard nut to crack. Or are you a nutcracker? [*Pause.*] Why are you staring at me like that?

DIANE: I'm not staring.

GILLIAN: Condescending.

TODD: [*offstage, calling*] Diane... Diane...

GILLIAN: You'd better go. It might be your father-in-law's last words.

DIANE *exits. A pensive* GILLIAN *tops up her drink.*

VOICE: [KEITH] He's a skeleton. That was sweet of you. I like golden pudding. Golden dumplings, a goldmine for you and you and you and you all want goldmines and you're devouring me. Pardon me, sir, how long will the train be? Seven carriages, sir. Pardon my sins.

Son, I'm dying. Yep, yep, yep, sirrie. You gotta get up early to catch the worm, because the worms turn if you're not up early. All right, sleep in. I can't sleep.

> GILLIAN *looks up at the ceiling, smiles to herself and suddenly sits on the floor. Then an idea occurs to her. She pretends to shoot herself in the head. She falls backwards in slow motion, as if she imagines herself in a film, and lies down on the floor.* LUKE *enters, wearing a new jacket, to get himself a drink. He doesn't see her.*

GILLIAN: I spy, with my little eye…

LUKE: [*noticing her*] Christ… for a moment I thought you were dead.

GILLIAN: Me back. Ricked it a few days ago giving Keith a blow job. Where'd you get the jacket?

LUKE: My wardrobe. Used to live here, in my own house. Funny but true. It's cold. You notice that?—Australian houses can be very cold, but European houses very warm. This house is cold. Like a morgue. Which is very appropriate.

GILLIAN: How's the boy?

LUKE: Looks worse than I thought.

GILLIAN: Yes, I think he's likely to pop off at any moment. [*Pause.*] What do you think?

LUKE: This tastes good. Didn't drink much alcohol when I was away. What do I think? Of what?

GILLIAN: Malcolm.

LUKE: What I said.

GILLIAN: Did you do any thinking about him—about you and him?

LUKE: I looked at him, if that's what you mean. I wish he'd been healthier.

GILLIAN: Why?

LUKE: So I could have hated him more. It's hard to hate something so porous.

GILLIAN: Porous?

LUKE: Yes, everything is pouring out of him. Piss and shit, only in the wrong orifices. Ray was right. We are only bags of shit, piss, water and sperm. And then there's the garbage of emotions.

GILLIAN: Speak for yourself.

LUKE: And ovaries—if you include the other gender.

Pause.

GILLIAN: Who's this Ray?

LUKE: Dad used him as a stand-over man, with the unions, that sort of thing.

GILLIAN: He certainly had a bleak view of humans.

LUKE: Yes, I think when he hurt or killed them he probably thought he was doing them a favour. He probably thought he was doing Esther a favour.

GILLIAN: What sort of favour?

LUKE: Did I say that? He did no one any favours. Didn't do me one.

Pause.

GILLIAN: You miss Esther still, don't you?

LUKE: Well, Gillian, it's like all the insides of my body have been removed and replaced with damp straw. I'm this scarecrow whose limbs shake in the wind to frighten everyone away. Boyce Park was built on the ashes of her body.

GILLIAN: Maybe the stars weren't aligned the right way for you and Esther.

LUKE: Astrology is for people too lazy to fathom the mysteries of astronomy.

Pause.

GILLIAN: There's no need to ridicule my beliefs.

LUKE: Why not? Astrology's stupid.

GILLIAN: It comforts me.

VOICE: [TODD] Chest-deep, going under... Ray of light... Save me... Banks... I'll get the money. Enchanted evening... across a crowded room full of... Pick up the piece of wood and hit him! Hit him hard and run... run as fast as you can, the gingerbread man...

LUKE: If, Gillian, if he hadn't have looked so pathetic I could have... done or said something to him. Hurt him. He just looked like a dying animal, an animal I didn't know. Sooooo, Gillian, it was very, very disappointing to me.

GILLIAN: You seem... a bit—

LUKE: Bit...?

GILLIAN: On something.

LUKE: Bitten.

Pause.

GILLIAN: That Diane dresses well, doesn't she? But as for those fuck-me shoes, must buy a pair for myself—even I want to fuck her. I wish I had the legs for really tiny miniskirts. It's so easy for a man to service you then. Bend over a little... whoops, he's in. So simple and convenient. This reminds me of being on my back in a pool. In a pool, Luke. I like swimming at night in water so cold it's like being immersed in a jungle of ice needles. The chandelier—looks like ice crystals, doesn't it?

LUKE: Yes, they do.

GILLIAN: Float on my back and look at the moon... I'm better at backstroke than the Australian crawl... maybe it's the term 'Australian crawl'—crawl before you can walk. You think a lot when you're on your back, which is why women think a lot. And when it's snowing you can swallow snowflakes. Listen to the palm trees, if you're in the tropics. Hmmmm, ambrosia wafting into my nostrils. Give me a hand, kind sir.

He helps her up.

LUKE: You want?

GILLIAN: I want.

He takes her glass and pours a drink for her.

What was it about Esther...? You could have had any girl. Me included, you know.

Pause.

LUKE: Really. Must tell Keith. I remember a story about a famous rock-and-roll group. The girl screwed all the members of the band before settling on one and marrying him. You of that ilk?

GILLIAN: Why did she choose the one particular guy?

LUKE: Lead singer, of course. No one's going to marry a bass player.

GILLIAN: [*taking the drink*] Thank you.

LUKE: That's what Mum keeps on saying—thank you, thank you.

GILLIAN: To whom?

LUKE: Dad. That's why I left the room. Couldn't stand it. He treated her... well, you know, abysmally. The coldness. The other women. Her loneliness. And now she says to him—thank you. For fucking what, Gillian? She wants him to survive and treat her like shit again?

GILLIAN: Maybe that's what it's about—she'd prefer that to being by herself.

LUKE: [*mimicking his mother*] Thank you, thank you, thank you...

GILLIAN: The meek, Luke, the meek do inherit the earth. Keith says to me—that I drain him of his strength and that he, the strong one, will be defeated by me, the meek. And, you know something? Keithie is right! [*A beat.*] Maybe your mother fed off Malcolm, like a parasite.

LUKE: For a person who knows fuck-all, you know fuck-all. Keith's right.

GILLIAN: Don't be cruel.

LUKE: Thank you, thank you, thank you.

VOICE: [KEITH] I'm leaving the room, got to get out of here, 'cause I know my way back. Most people, most people are clowns, most clowns wouldn't have the fucking sense to get back in the room after they got out. I'm no clown. You're a clown.

LUKE: How long have you been out, Gillian?

GILLIAN: Short visit this time. It's necessary for both me and Keith. Do you know what he says: 'A mad woman is a tautology'. But then I hear these voices when it gets bad. 'You've got to listen to us', 'To hell with you', 'Okay, then, if you don't like me, I'll go'. Weird, eh?

LUKE: Have you always heard them?

GILLIAN: No. Everything began in rage. When I set fire to my bedroom, I was probably about thirteen. I was in this rage. Rage is what teenage girls do well, because there doesn't seem a reason for it. I thought, 'Hello, maybe I've gone a bit too far'. Then I threw a chair at my mother—no wonder we were estranged. I did modern dance as therapy. Given that modern dance had no structure and can be anything you like, it did me more harm than good. What I mean is that it's so easy to think you can do it after years of not doing it. So, I was in the santo and I thought I'd dance. It wasn't a blow job. I did my back in, doing modern dance. Luke, sometimes it's so wonderful. When the madness begins to hit me, it's like I'm possessed by euphoria... Oh, the epiphanies. I see the meaning of life, I see myself dancing, the greatest dancer in the world, I see the meaning, the meaning of everything and that's so thrilling because life is so meaningless. My *grand behaviour*. How terrible and wonderful it is—and all the time I am *high maintenance*. *Very high maintenance.* Beyond happiness into another realm of ecstasy and then... whoomp! From the top of the mountain to the bottom of the crevasse. Nurses, lawns, slow-moving people talking to themselves, others wiping their shit on the walls and the cottonwool mind of medication. But no daytime TV soaps!

LUKE: [*laughing*] No, that would mean—

GILLIAN: Gone. Fully gone. And your epilepsy? Gone?

LUKE: I had one bad attack. No, it was a good attack. I woke up and thought Esther was still alive and I was talking to her, but it was only her ghost. So, good and bad. And since then—no hint of it.

GILLIAN: Maybe it was all the dope in Amsterdam?

Pause.

LUKE: Venice, you mean.

GILLIAN: No, Amsterdam. News gets around.

LUKE: Amsterdam, what can I tell you about it? I think I saw some movies, woke up in some strange places and there were times when I swear I could understand and communicate in Dutch, but I was merely talking double-dutch.

Pause.

GILLIAN: Did it help?

LUKE: It was good. I could talk to Esther as if she were with me. Because, really, no one, no one can prepare you for grief. No one. It's like peering into an infinite chasm. No bottom. Not even echoes. But in Amsterdam I had this sense there was an afterlife. There had to be an afterlife or love didn't make sense. One early morning I found myself in a park and it was cold, bitterly cold, but I didn't feel it. And it occurred to me that love is the soul. If we've never loved, then we have no soul. Once I thought that, I knew it was time to come back.

GILLIAN: Very romantic, Luke.

LUKE: So there had to be an afterlife. And this is the best thing—when she left me that morning, I was still stoned enough not to grieve her going. Epilepsy gone too. Venice is not good for one who is grieving. It's like a giant, watery graveyard. It took drugs, but I was happy in Amsterdam. Artificial happiness is not to be gainsaid.

GILLIAN: I've been happy recently. As recent as yesterday. You know what perked me up yesterday? Made me happy for the whole day? I walked out of your parents' room and was coming downstairs when I heard what sounded like someone in pain. The noise was coming from the room next to theirs. It was Diane and Todd having sex. After coming out of a room filled with death it was fantastic to hear sex. I've heard that someone dying makes the living randy. And it's true.

LUKE: It's true? [*Pause.*] I am not randy.

GILLIAN: I would have liked to have watched them.

KEITH: [*entering*] What's that?

GILLIAN: Diane and Todd having sex yesterday.

KEITH: I think I'll pass on that one. I mean... that woman. It's like she owns him.

GILLIAN: Todd?

KEITH: He's cunt-struck. As for Dad. She holds his hands, whispers in his ear... You'd think she was his daughter. [*He goes to get a drink.*] Drink, darling?

GILLIAN: Hmmm, sounds like Keith could be randy. Yes, darling. Luke now believes in the afterlife.

KEITH: That's a horrible thought, Luke. That means that Dad will live to haunt us. He's always been threatening to do that.

GILLIAN: You don't believe in the afterlife, darling?

KEITH: God knows, life is terrible enough. Death is God's punishment for us being born. To give us an afterlife would be too much punishment.

GILLIAN: You don't think you're paranoiac about her?

KEITH: Diane? She unnerves me. Always seems to be calculating.

GILLIAN: About what?

> KEITH *shrugs and gives her the drink.*

You don't want to share your paranoia with me? I can tell you one thing, though—and only another women can say this with all certainty—she fakes her orgasms. [*Pause.*] You know, darling, what I've just learnt from Luke? [*Pause.*] I have no soul.

KEITH: I wonder if Gillian fakes her orgasms? I must get a woman in to watch me and Gillian have sex so she can tell me. What do you think, darling?

GILLIAN: Ah, the male fantasy of the ménage à trois.

KEITH: [to LUKE, *as he goes to get himself a drink*] Every time I have sex with my wife it's like I'm committing an act of necrophilia. [*As he pours himself a drink*] What does Gillian mean, she has no soul?

LUKE: Perhaps she hasn't.

KEITH: Typical. Typical.

LUKE: [*to* GILLIAN] The latest retreat seems to have done you some good.

KEITH: It's not the times in the sanatoriums. It's the day-to-day stuff recently. When she's well—and when she's well, then things go like this. I arrive home and she's stoned and pissed. And happy, may I say, so there's something to be said for drugs and booze. So she asks me about my day and I tell her. After I've finished, she says to me, 'Well, tell me about your day'. She's forgotten what I've said. Or I'll tell her we're going out the following evening and she's surprised next day when I ask her what she's going to wear. 'First time I've heard about it,' she says. I arrive home to pick her up to take her out and she's got this wonky smile and her eyes are bloodshot with dope, and we go out and she stumbles around the rooms, crashing into things, smashing things and falling over. Those are our nights out. Next day she wakes up really cheery having forgotten the evening completely.

GILLIAN: It helps me get into party mode. At least I mix with people. Why don't you mix with others at parties?

KEITH: I do. But I like to talk.

GILLIAN: At least dance. You look like a wooden Indian nickel.

KEITH: Wooden Indian.

GILLIAN: You wandered around the wedding reception like you had a broom handle stuck up your arse.

KEITH: Metaphorically you placed it there. But, I mean, who can criticise Miss here when she has no memory of what she did at a party, and even when I tell her what she did, she has no sense of embarrassment? Do you, Gillian? I used to be embarrassed by her stoned and drunken behaviour, but now I just float above it. Can't stand, however, those looks of sympathy everyone gives me and, may I say, those disapproving looks strangers give me when we're out and she's got two black eyes because she's fallen over or walked into a wall or a sculpture.

GILLIAN: Those modern sculptures have lots of pointy bits.

LUKE: Isn't she seeing a psychiatrist?

GILLIAN: I'm here. I'm here!

KEITH: For years, the same one. I asked her what she talks about. Me, she said, and sometimes you. That made me shudder. There's nothing more brutal and clinical than a woman dissecting the weaknesses of her husband, unless she's talking about her ex-husband. One day I was having a business meeting in the same building where her headshrinker has an office. I'm in the lift and this woman—big, blonde hair, big tits—the psychiatrist—Gillian had described her well—

GILLIAN: It's difficult having a psychiatrist that looks like Jayne Mansfield, it helps me to feel sexually inadequate.

KEITH: She hops into the lift and is on her mobile. I thought I might introduce myself. Let her know I don't have horns, rabies and the mind of a serial rapist, but she's on the mobile shouting at some

Sibylla Budd as Gillian and Toby Schmitz as Luke in the 2006 Griffin Theatre Company production of THE EMPEROR OF SYDNEY. (Photo: Robert McFarlane)

poor idiot at the funeral home for overcharging her thirty dollars for her mother's funeral. Thirty dollars! And the next call she makes is to a department store savaging them for not giving her bras the same size. She gets out at her floor and is still haranguing the sales girl, yelling at her, 'My tits need special care. Not that you would know, you flat-chested wonder!' Gillian's headshrinker—mad as a cut snake. No wonder Gillian never seems to make progress. I thought she had a good point about her tits, though. Massive. You'd need a water bag, a compass and abseiling gear just to explore them. They should be cared for. If you were a male client it'd be hard not to have a hard-on when you told her your sexual fantasies. But arguing over thirty dollars for her mother's funeral... what kind of...?

LUKE: Reminds me, what are we going to do about him?

KEITH: All taken care of. Diane has had intimate chats with Mum and they've decided on a funeral at St Mary's.

LUKE: But it's the biggest church in Sydney. Who's going to turn up?

KEITH: Hundreds who will want proof that he's dead. Diane used to be an actress, so she must know he'll get a full house.

LUKE: But St Mary's is Catholic.

KEITH: Apparently Diane and Mum have interpreted Dad's delirium as a newly-discovered belief in God and his Catholic upbringing.

LUKE: You can say what you like about Dad—but he's a fucking atheist. The most godless man I have ever known. Even if there were a God, Dad wouldn't believe in Him because he couldn't believe there was room enough for two Gods in the world.

KEITH: Diane insists and, Luke, let me say, that when Diane insists, there is little opportunity to say no. He's going to be embalmed.

LUKE: He'd hate that.

KEITH: Open casket. And can you see it, Luke? Can you fucking see it? Diane bending over the coffin kissing him, pausing to whisper something to him. Something we can't hear and everyone in the church thinking: God, they must have been close. And her face will be shiny with tears and there'll be a weak' smile of regret, love, secrets she's shared with him. And the fucking kid crying just so we notice the grandson.

LUKE: I'm looking forward to the performance.

GILLIAN: Are you sure you're not keen on Diane?

KEITH: Ever since Todd's been with her and come back into the family, it's like he's cock of the walk. And there'll be reporters there, so she'll have a fashionable black hat, sunglasses. And the reporters will do stories about us tearing each other apart over the spoils. They'll write these stupid stories.

LUKE: They're people without a soul.

KEITH: Who?

LUKE: A reporter is a writer without a soul. So they'll fill up the vacuum, where their soul should be, with bile. You know why they hate us? Because they envy us. They want what we have. That's why they're always doing those garbage stories about us.

GILLIAN *starts to exit.*

KEITH: Where are you going?

GILLIAN: Upstairs.

KEITH: What? With that drink?

GILLIAN: What's your problem, darling? Your dad going to cark it because I'm having a drink? Drink is life: I'm drinking to life. It helps calm me as I'm watching him die.

GILLIAN *exits and an irritated* KEITH *studies the model.*

VOICE: [LUKE] Lord, Lord, Lord. Lord have mercy on me. Good Lord! Good Lord, one more moment, a long, long moment, O Lord. How can I stand this? I am sitting up for you, O Lord. Help me, help me this evening. I happen to be one. Yes, sirrie, O Lord, I am a sinner. Take good aim, nurse. Get the vein. Take good aim with a fucking lump of wood on my dad's noggin. Then run! Run, run, as fast as you can. I'm the gingerbread man.

KEITH: You haven't kept a close eye on this, have you?

LUKE: It seems to be well-made.

KEITH: The whole project.

LUKE: The bank gave Dad the money and the project's going ahead.

KEITH: While you've been away certain things have been happening. I've been guilty of not keeping a close eye on it. There's been Gillian's latest bout and that housing project out west.

LUKE: The barns for breeders?

KEITH: Our bread and butter. Lots of money in it. Look at that stupid neon. Boyce. Boyce. Boyce.

LUKE: What was Dad thinking?

KEITH: You mean, what was Todd thinking? [*Motioning to the rooms in the model*] You notice the colour scheme?

LUKE: No.

KEITH: Todd has arranged for the interior decor to be changed. I only found out when one of the construction firms told me.

LUKE: And Dad agreed? He knows nothing about interior design. He basically says, 'Leave it up to those poofters'.

KEITH: Well, this time he's left it up to Todd. Which has been bothering me. Who's going to run the firm once Dad's gone?

LUKE: The three of us.

KEITH: How?

LUKE: I don't know, I haven't thought about it.

KEITH: How, Luke? Dad ran it as a one-man show. If we're all given the same responsibilities, how will we run it?

LUKE: He told me once that he was giving the company to the three of us.

KEITH: You don't feel that's a recipe for disaster?

    LUKE *peers in at the rooms.*

VOICE: [TODD] Come on, you know it's time to go home.

VOICE: [KEITH] Coming, Mummy. I'm going to need a little assistance, no fucking hospital for me and a hospice filled with the walking dead. Dead man walking! There must be more than nothing. Half the time she doesn't know we are in the room. I am going into the jungle, I may be some time. Black as a nigger, I was. Burnt black working in the sun. The sun, I was.

LUKE: The rooms don't look too bad.

KEITH: That's not the point. Todd did it to me without telling us. So, is that the way the company's going to work?

LUKE: Let's kill the fucker!

    Pause.

KEITH: It's serious. The press is salivating over this. Everyday stories about the dying titan, dying self-made man, a construction giant… So, who's he going to give the real power to?

LUKE: He told me—us three. He told you.

VOICE: [TODD] She died, burning like a witch. She wanted to destroy me. She was a witch burning in hell…

KEITH: It won't work, Luke. Somehow Diane's convinced Dad that Todd's special. The black sheep has returned home to become the only ram in the paddock. You know, I haven't been here while Dad's been dying without Todd or Diane being in that room, hovering over him like fucking vultures.

LUKE: What about this house?

KEITH: He's left it to Mum until she dies and then we three share it.

LUKE: Share it? How do we do that?

KEITH: Sell it and share the money, I guess. I haven't actually seen the will. He's just told me the main stuff. This damn neon sign. That's Todd appealing to Dad's ego. Boyce Park was once going to be discreet words in wrought iron on the front gate and now it's like we're giving the one-finger salute to the whole of Sydney.

LUKE *stares at the name on the model.*

VOICE: [LUKE] I didn't blink! I didn't blink! You blinked. You blinked!

KEITH: The problem is, Luke, our name will become a burden.

LUKE: It already has.

LUKE *pours a drink for himself and* KEITH.

VOICE: [TODD] Oh, love me.

VOICE: [KEITH] Build it!

VOICE: [LUKE] Don't let that woman stop us!

VOICE: [KEITH] How long does it take to drive there? How long does it take to drive here?

VOICE: [LUKE] We'll take both roads.

VOICE: [KEITH] Son, you look so well. You know what your mother's hobby is—?

VOICE: [LUKE] To tell everyone they look well.

VOICE: [KEITH] You see, I can't tell when I'm dead.

VOICE: [LUKE] Am I dead? You see, I can't tell.

VOICE: [TODD] The guy who shot Doc Holliday, he was the bravest of them all.

TODD *enters.*

LUKE: Ah, Toddy… [*Re: the drink*] A splash?

TODD: No. No, thank you, Lukie.

Pause.

KEITH: Dad?

TODD: Getting worse.

KEITH: How long?

TODD: The nurse is calling the doctor. [*Pause.*] I was wondering if you wanted to say any final words to him?

KEITH: I did.

TODD: What did you say?

KEITH: Private.

> *Pause.*

TODD: Luke?

LUKE: Hurry up and die, you fucker, would be pretty much my final words to him—Toddy.

> *Pause.*

TODD: It's Todd. [*To* KEITH] And it's Diane, not Di.

KEITH: She doesn't seem to mind.

TODD: She told you she does, so why not call her by the name she wants to be called? I could call your wife Gilly instead of Gillian.

KEITH: Why don't you?

> *Pause.*

TODD: Our father's dying up there.

LUKE: So?

TODD: Respect for him, respect for me, respect for my wife.

KEITH: Don't you have to earn respect?

TODD: What in the fuck does that mean?

KEITH: Can I make it plainer, Luke?

LUKE: As plain and as straightforward as the sign on the front of this. [*Pause.*] I gather you had the interiors changed?

TODD: I would have told you, but you were in Venice, or was that Amsterdam?

LUKE: Right on both counts. I can understand I was very difficult to track down to get my opinion on the colour of the bathroom walls... so I am not having a go at you.

TODD: You were overseas, Keith was up to his neck with that housing estate project and I was spending a lot of time listening to people you were considering buying in. The interiors were too stark. The colours had to be warmer. The bathrooms and kitchens less, you know, industrial. It's not the outside of the building, just the interiors. It's not such a big thing. As you know, Keith—did you tell Luke this?—once the changes were made we've practically sold every apartment off the plan. It's paid for itself many times over.

KEITH: I would have liked to have been consulted, that's all.

TODD: You were too busy and, don't forget, Keith, I wouldn't have made such a decision if I hadn't asked Dad's opinion. He's still running the company.

KEITH: Is he?

TODD: If he hadn't have agreed, it wouldn't have happened.

KEITH: He doesn't know what he's doing. One moment he's talking about playing on the railway tracks as a kid and the next he's saying how he works like a nigger.

TODD: He was lucid when he agreed. That was weeks back. It's not now. I knew how much this project meant to him. He told me over and over. Fuck, how many times did the architect have to change plans because of the environmental laws, the protests against it, the costs just to lay the first brick—?

KEITH: To get his monument.

TODD: Yes, to get his monument. This is already being written about as a classic piece of contemporary living space.

LUKE: You sound like an advertisement.

TODD: I understand this building, Luke. I studied interior design.

LUKE: You didn't finish the course—like Diane.

Pause.

TODD: I know enough to appreciate what's good, what's bad. Do you, Luke? I'd like to live in that.

LUKE: Something that's built on someone's ashes?

TODD: You argue like a woman. I'm only talking about the architecture.

LUKE: I argue like a woman? One with PMT or just the usual feminine lack of logic?

KEITH: Or Di's logic? Diane's logic.

TODD: Christ... face it. I changed things and it worked. This project could have been our end, now it's a new beginning for the Boyce name. [To LUKE] And you, you'd gone walkabout. Even if I had gotten hold of you, what sort of interior did you want? Psychedelic colours?

LUKE: I assume you're referring to my sojourn in the Land of Soma. Boy, word gets around.

GILLIAN *enters.*

GILLIAN: I really need a top-up now.

KEITH: Why?

Pause.

GILLIAN: He's gone.

TODD: He's dead?

GILLIAN: Yes, your father's dead.

Pause.

TODD: I'd better—

GILLIAN: No, stay down here. Your mum wants to be left alone with the body for a while.

TODD: Where's Diane?

GILLIAN: In the bathroom. She'll be down in a moment.

Silence.

KEITH: Todd, a drink now?

TODD: Yes, please.

Silence as KEITH *makes him a drink and silently offers to do the same for* GILLIAN *and* LUKE, *both of whom nod in agreement.*

Were you there?

GILLIAN: Yes. Me, Diane, your mum and the nurse. The nurse is making arrangements for the ambulance and stuff like that.

KEITH: How did he go?

GILLIAN: He was muttering weird things as usual.

LUKE: What was he saying?

GILLIAN: Nonsense. Nothing about you. He said something about burning a witch and about Doc Holliday or something.

LUKE: Hope my last words are more profound than that.

GILLIAN: Then he went quiet. I thought he was asleep. The nurse checked his pulse and he lay down as if asleep and then, just when we thought it was all over, he suddenly arched backwards, sat up and exhaled—as if his spirit left him—and then he fell back.

KEITH: What do you mean, his spirit left him?

GILLIAN: That's what it seemed like. When he fell back his body was just a shell.

Pause.

LUKE: And Mum? How did she take this?

GILLIAN: She wept. She's holding his hand now, stroking his brow, talking to him.

TODD: Diane?

GILLIAN: Cried too. I did a little too. He looked so empty all of a sudden.

TODD: I should have been there.

GILLIAN: He just went, Todd. None of us knew it was going to be then.

> DIANE *enters. She has composed herself but is still cut up about it.* TODD *hugs her.*

DIANE: I'm sorry. I'm sorry, Todd. God, I hate death.

TODD: It's all right, baby. Baby, it's all right.

KEITH: We're having a drink, Diane.

DIANE: That would be good.

> *An awkward silence as* KEITH *fills a glass and hands it to* DIANE.

Your mum wants to be—

GILLIAN: I told them.

TODD: How long does she want to be alone?

DIANE: Just give me some time, she said.

> *Silence.*

LUKE: What did you think, Diane, when your father-in-law suddenly sat up and took his last breath? A little scared?

GILLIAN: He didn't take his last breath. He exhaled. It left him.

DIANE: His soul left him.

LUKE: He had a soul? That I find spooky.

> *Silence.*

DIANE: Anybody going to say something? You respected him? Loved him? Going to miss him? [*Pause.*] A man just died up there. Your flesh and blood, Todd.

TODD: I know. I'm getting used to the idea.

DIANE: Used to the idea?

TODD: I'm trying to take it in…

LUKE: It means you're free.

TODD: It means no such thing. He was just a… force of nature. I never thought he'd die. It was like he was bigger than death.

GILLIAN: [*indicating he should say something*] Keith…
KEITH: Me?

> GILLIAN *nods.*

[*Ruefully*] Don't think I haven't thought about this moment. [*To everyone*] The first point is that [*referring to* LUKE *and* TODD] if it wasn't for him, we wouldn't be here. Obvious, I know. The second thing is that we must help Mum. God knows, she's going to miss him. And the third, a toast to a man whom, for all his imperfections, did create an empire. Not many men can say that. To our father. To Malcolm.
ALL: [*toasting*] To Malcolm.

> *Pause.*

DIANE: That's it?
KEITH: Can't do better than Todd—he was a force of nature. If I had known I would have written a speech. I could have mentioned toilets.
TODD: Pride in toilets.

> KEITH, LUKE *and* TODD *laugh.*

DIANE: [*to* TODD] What's the matter with you three?
TODD: The soul of a building—
KEITH: —is in its toilets.
LUKE: You can tell how proud a company is—
TODD: —by looking at the dunnies.
KEITH: In toilets you can smell the pride of a company—
TODD: —their attitude. [*To* DIANE] That was one of my first lessons. Keith was taught first, then me, then Luke. Dad would enter a big company and go and have a pee in the workers' toilets. If they were dirty and smelly, he would have nothing to do with the company. He'd drag us into all these toilets and tell us the financial prospects of the company just by the state of their dunnies.
KEITH: Now, that's a telling moment, how we remember our dad— toilets.
LUKE: I've been in more toilets than a rent boy.
KEITH: Maybe at the church service I can mention his theory about toilets—given that our father never believed in God and is going to have a funeral in a place he despised.

DIANE: He changed his mind about the funeral. That's what dying does to you.

KEITH: Did he change his mind, Todd?

DIANE: He told me. He told your mother.

LUKE: Can't I go up there and put a stake through his heart just to make sure?

GILLIAN: Luke...

DIANE: He just died, for goodness sake.

LUKE: Don't lecture me about my own father.

TODD: Luke, allow her to be upset, even if you're not.

LUKE: Diane. Would you be upset if your father died?

TODD: Just leave it alone.

DIANE: No, I wouldn't, Luke. He was everything I wanted my father to be.

LUKE: Now, that's upsetting

KEITH: Todd's right, Luke... it's too raw. Too early.

LUKE: Thank you, thank you, thank you.

> *Pause.*

DIANE: I just don't think one should speak ill of the dead.

LUKE: Did you read that on a greeting card?

TODD: This is my wife—

DIANE: It's okay, I can look after myself. Your father was just a human being, we all have our flaws.

LUKE: He was just a human being—what kind of nonsense is that? Human being were created by God when he was on bad drugs.

DIANE: If that's your view, then you're not fit to judge human beings.

LUKE: Oh, but I do judge my father, Diane. And I have every right to.

GILLIAN: I saw a lot of his good side, okay?

TODD: Dad put his hand up your dress and feel your pussy too?

GILLIAN: No one, including Keith, has done it for so long... Why, did Malcolm make a habit of it, Todd?

DIANE: Todd's trying to be funny.

GILLIAN: Oh, I don't know. I've always suspected that Malcolm was a womaniser, a wascal.

KEITH: Wascal. Oh, baby talk. Gillian's father was a wascal. He told me—first and only time I ever met him—that he had screwed six hundred and eight women. And two sets of mothers and daughters.

Wonderful example, I must follow it to get into Gillian's good books. He was a teacher of maths, so I trust his figures. Gillian admired him. Many women like womanisers. They think a womaniser loves women. They don't. A womaniser is merely drunk on cunt. Just like an alcoholic wants booze. Dad was a womaniser.

TODD: I don't think he was. I think he kept a mistress.

KEITH: What do you think, Luke?

LUKE: She was his mistress.

KEITH: Who?

LUKE: Esther.

DIANE: The woman who died?

LUKE: [*motioning to the model*] Yes, the woman who died for that. Esther was Dad's mistress.

> *Pause.*

TODD: That's bullshit. It's not true. That's pushing too far, Luke.

> *Pause.*

KEITH: You're kidding?

LUKE: The body's barely cold upstairs. Would I kid about this? I didn't find out until after she died. She had been his mistress before we met.

> GILLIAN *laughs.*

DIANE: What's so funny?

GILLIAN: The same mistress.

> *She laughs again and* KEITH *automatically takes the glass from her and fills it up.*

[*Laughing*] Fuck me dead. Fuck me dead...

KEITH: Careful for what you ask, Gillian.

LUKE: It was certainly a surprise, Gillian. But when I was in Venice something struck me. I hadn't truly absorbed the fact—father and son had the same mistress—until one night when I had been in Venice for a couple of days. I was walking back to my apartment— amazing how ghostly Venice is at night because all the workers go back to the mainland and the *palazzi* are empty waiting for their American owners to come in the summer—and I was walking back through a narrow *calle* near a canal, and I realised I was lost and

couldn't find my way back to the hotel. I heard two women speaking
in the Venetian dialect—it sounds like sing-song—and their voices
echoed everywhere, and I didn't know where they were, and then
they came out of nowhere, a very attractive mother and daughter
arm-in-arm. The thought struck me. What if I had had an affair with
a mother and a daughter? When I was making love to the daughter
would I have detected similarities to the mother—the voice, the
noises she makes in sex, her figure, the shape of her breasts...?
Would I have gotten off on that? Did Esther get off on the fact that
she had father and then the son? Did I remind her of him? Something
in my voice was familiar? The way I made love? The same sort
of phrases? The same sort of sweet nothings? Did I say the same
things as Dad when I was having sex with her? Did she close her
eyes and say to herself when I was inside her, 'Like father, like son.
They have exactly the same grunts when they're pushing into me.
Oh yes, they both like to lick me behind me ears.' You can imagine
my thoughts. Well, perhaps only men can. And when she saw the
similarity, was she appalled or did it excite her to recognise the
same things in the both of us? And it hit me so hard—that if she had
seen the similarities, then it meant I had not escaped him. I was a
part of him as he was a part of me. I stood there in the freezing cold,
thinking back. I was jealous if she told me about any of her lovers
and one day she said she would tell me about the married man who
had kept her. I told her not to. Thank fucking goodness she didn't
tell me. I tried to remember what she said about me that made me
different. I remember us sitting on the balcony having a drink and
I saw her soft belly and I touched it, wanting to feel it. It was so
feminine, so soft, and she said, 'Do you think I've put on too much
weight?' Did Dad ever touch her like I did—with such absolute love
and adoration? Did she ever give the same reply? I couldn't move.
Some tourists passed me and must have thought I looked like a real
eejit standing there near the canal lost in thought but, you see, I had
to remember if she said anything that made me different from Dad,
that made me more special than him, and I remember the last time
we were together and she said, 'You make me happy', and once I
remembered those words, then I knew he had made her sad. I was
the better man. I had made her happy.

DIANE: So that's the reason you hate him—the father-son sexual rivalry?

LUKE: Where do you get your platitudes from—reality TV shows?

TODD *goes to defend* DIANE *but she holds her hand up to stop him.*

DIANE: I touched something raw.

GILLIAN: [*still amused*] But how did it happen? How did you end up sharing a mistress with Malcolm?

LUKE: Sharing isn't the word. When I fell for Esther I didn't know she had been Dad's mistress. And when she died the thing that struck me the most about Dad, you know, the dead man up there, was that he would have the woman, who had been his mistress for nearly a decade, killed.

TODD: He didn't have her killed.

LUKE: What would you know? [*Pause. Realising*] You knew. You fucking knew!

DIANE: Knew what?

LUKE: You knew, Todd. He told you before she died.

DIANE: You knew, Todd?

Pause.

TODD: Everyone knew that this Tucker woman was photogenic, articulate, and she had the newspapers on her side. An alone woman trying to protect the environment while the evil Boyces wanted to destroy it with their project. What a combination. Brilliant. How could we compete with that? I didn't know it at the time, but little Luke put up his hand and said, 'I'll talk to her. I'm so handsome. Everyone loves me. I'll turn her around. I'm Luke, I'm God's gift to women—this'll be easy as pie.' And then he fell in love with her. Didn't even attempt to change her mind. So she continued her attacks on us. We were facing ruin.

LUKE: You're not telling me something important, Todd. Todd!

TODD: Dad had cancer. He knew he only had months to live. This project was his dream. No one could laugh at him for cheap housing anymore. I'd see him every day at work. He'd be lost in thought... He couldn't believe why Tucker was doing this to him. That's what he said to me one day when I asked him about it. He said it was a personal vendetta against him. I asked him why and he said he didn't know.

LUKE: Didn't know? Really? That's all he said about her?

TODD: He said he didn't know. But now I know more about her, then maybe Dad was right. It *was* personal. He had left Esther and her revenge was to destroy us, pretending all the time that she was concerned about what we would do to the environment.

LUKE: She believed in what she was fighting for.

TODD: See, still on her side. She played you, Luke.

LUKE: She loved me.

TODD: I don't know if she did, but it sounds as if she had you by the balls.

LUKE: She has me by everything, Todd. My balls... my heart.

TODD: Dad said to me, 'I want your advice'. It was the first time ever in my life he had asked my advice. It was then he told me about you. He said you had chosen that woman over family.

LUKE: Did he tell you about a stand-over guy called Ray?

TODD: He said he didn't know what to do about you and that, in times of trouble with the unions and the like, he had used this stand-over fellow, Ray Pollard, to, you know, talk some sense into them.

LUKE: A stand-over man talking sense... And Dad asked your advice?

TODD: Yes. He said I was the only son he could trust. So I gave him my advice.

LUKE: For Ray to have a 'chat' with Esther?

TODD: Convince her.

LUKE: Do you know what the word convince meant to Ray? He killed her, Todd.

TODD: He didn't kill her. She died in a fire. The police confirmed it.

LUKE: Ray was a pyromaniac. He knew how to make a house fire look like an accident. You know what happened, Todd? After taking your advice, Ray visited Esther. He lost his temper, belted her across the head and she fell and cracked her skull and died. So he set fire to the house.

GILLIAN: How do you know this?

LUKE: I asked Ray. He was in a hospice. He did love something in his life—his parrots. He liked to kiss them and they gave him avian flu. What a fucking stupid way to die. I spoke to him just before he died. He had no reason to lie to me. He was very good at convincing people. Killing Esther was some fucking convincing, don't you think, Todd?

TODD: I just gave advice to Dad. She had pushed us into a corner. I assumed—

LUKE: Assumed?

TODD: —that this Ray fellow was going to scare her into giving up the protest, that's all.

LUKE: Did you have any idea of how he was going to scare her? Like, put on an Osama bin Laden mask and jump out of a bush? Make bloodcurdling noises outside her window? [*Pause.*] Answer me, you cunt.

TODD: I thought he was going to talk to her—

LUKE: Hello, Esther, how are you? I would appreciate it if you gave up the protest—

TODD: Let me finish. You want the truth, I'll tell you. I knew he would have to confront her and scare her.

LUKE: And she'd give in?

TODD: Yes.

LUKE: Ray was a psychopath.

TODD: I didn't know that. Dad said he had done a lot of work for him, that's all.

LUKE: Dirty work.

TODD: Dirty work. It's the construction business, you know that.

LUKE: And that's the advice you gave Dad? Let Ray convince Esther to give up.

TODD: You didn't do your job. Someone had to convince her.

LUKE: [*referring to the model*] This is built on her ashes. She's going to haunt this building. She's going to bring it bad luck.

GILLIAN: Luke…

LUKE: Fuck it, I'm going to show you what you did to her.

> LUKE *goes to smash the model but* TODD *grabs him and pins him against the wall.*

TODD: Don't you lay a fucking finger on it.

LUKE: Mind the suit, man.

TODD: [*putting a hand around his throat*] Shut up! Shut the fuck up!

DIANE: Todd—

TODD: Be quiet.

KEITH: Todd, let him go.

TODD: Stay out of this, Keith, or I'll fucking come at you too. [*To* LUKE] I helped save us. When Dad told me about Esther he asked my advice and I knew that because you had only ever loved yourself that if you fell in love with someone else you would love her with the same intensity as you loved yourself. And would betray us. Because you are all that matters.

He lets LUKE *go.*

Keith doesn't know you like I do. Mum adored you. And you had your fits, which made her love you even more. I hated you and your seizures. I'd pick up the approaching fit by the expression on your face. I'd run around behind you. When you'd collapse, I'd cushion your fall and stretch you out on the floor, then clear all the furniture. You were the precious one. The Ming vase of the family. And despite this, you betrayed us. You loved Esther more than you loved your family. [*Pause.*] I have no regrets about the advice I gave, sonny boy. [*Motioning to the model*] You touch that and I'll kill you. That is my salvation. Dad gave me a chance. One last chance and I'm taking it.

KEITH: Taking it? Taking what? Dad gave you a chance? He treated you like shit. God, remember that time you climbed up a tree and couldn't get down? Dad told you to jump into his arms and he'd catch you. You were frightened and he said, 'Jump—you can trust me'. You jumped and he stepped away. You almost broke your legs and then he tells you, 'To trust is fine, not to trust is even better'. And you trust him to give you another chance?

TODD: Marrying Diane, having our boy—things changed. At the wedding he said to me that if our mother loved me then I was worthy of love and so he loved me through her. When he was dying he said that he loved me. He's a part of me.

LUKE: Like a virus?

TODD: Always the smart-arse.

LUKE: That was no spirit or soul that left him. He's inside me. He's not like some bloody worm-like alien about to burst out of my chest and leave me alone. It's more terrible than that. I can't get rid of him. He's the DNA in my fingernails, in my blood, my retina. Do I see like he does? He's in my sweat. My brain cells. My sperm. I have this one great justified fear that I'll end up being a genetic echo of him. That's why I am never going to have children. I don't want to pass on my genes. And you stand there and are proud that you will.

TODD: Yes, I am. I fought it practically all of my life, but I realised that I am he, he is me. When he grabbed my hand last night I felt this charge, his power going into me. Like an electric bolt, straight into me.

Pause.

KEITH: You cunt.

TODD: What's with you?

KEITH: I know where this is leading.

TODD: He said, 'I'm entrusting you to run the company. Not Keith. Not Luke. But you, Todd.'

Pause.

KEITH: Anyone else hear these words?

Pause.

DIANE: I did.

KEITH *gives an incredulous laugh.*

GILLIAN: Malcolm said that Todd was to run the business?

DIANE: Yes.

GILLIAN: Those were his words?

TODD: He said Keith didn't have the vision.

KEITH: Vision?

TODD: [*referring to the model*] You wanted to stop this.

KEITH: It was sending us broke.

TODD: But it didn't. It's made us again. This is what I am going to do—

KEITH: [*to* DIANE] I have never believed a word you have ever said. Even your lies are lies.

DIANE: It's the truth.

KEITH: It's hearsay.

GILLIAN: What are you talking about?

KEITH: It would never hold up in court. The will gives us a third each in the company.

TODD: And Mum gets the house until she dies. Yes, I know all that. I also know that I get to run the company.

LUKE: And I know why. It's not their kid, Keith—and it's not Diane. It's the convincing. When Dad asked you what should be done about Esther, you knew exactly what the words 'convince her' meant.

TODD: We talked about this before.

LUKE: It's the secret.

TODD: What secret?

LUKE: Once you agreed with Dad to 'convince' her, he must have been thrilled. He must have looked at you long and hard and then said to himself, 'Well, well, Todd does have a ruthless streak. He is quite prepared to hurt people in order to get what he wants. He's *the* son. He's the one son out of three who really is a chip off the old block.' And you saw the respect in his eyes. It was the first time you saw he had ever respected you. And you, Todd, thought to yourself, 'My God, I can be ruthless. I am a Boyce. I am my father's son.' From then on, Dad and you had a secret pact—

TODD: We had no such thing.

LUKE: I don't mean a written pact. Just the secret, unspoken knowledge that he and you both saw you as his successor. Agreeing to 'convince' Esther made you.

TODD: Too much dope in Amsterdam, Luke.

Alex Dimitriades (background) as Todd and Jack Finsterer as Keith in the 2006 Griffin Theatre Company production of THE EMPEROR OF SYDNEY. *(Photo: Robert McFarlane)*

LUKE: I must say I am surprised by that ruthless streak in you as much as probably Dad was. But I am not surprised at your behaviour now. Because it's driven by the slow-burning resentment of the perpetual underdog.

GILLIAN: Luke's right, Todd.

DIANE: I think this is between the sons.

GILLIAN: We are all family, Diane. You made that clear.

Pause.

KEITH: Luke and I will take you to court.

TODD: Luke won't. Luke is torn. Torn to bits, and nothing will put him back together again.

DIANE: A court case would destroy him.

KEITH: I will fight you, then.

TODD: Don't you two get it? This building is called Boyce. I am Boyce. My child is Boyce. Dad is in me and my boy. You two are dead-ends.

KEITH: How dare you! How dare this bitch and you think you can lie and take over.

TODD: I've got everything going for me, Keith. I'd win in court. Diane will confirm what he said and it will make perfect sense to a judge that a dying father would want the only grandson to carry on his name, to run the company. [*Pause.*] This is the deal—

KEITH: Deal? Luke and I worked with Dad, all you did was screw up. [*To* DIANE] You have put him up to this. You made sure you got pregnant and then you brought him and Dad together. You've fucking made it, Di.

TODD: Any more attacks on Diane and I'll slam you, Keith. Pick on me, don't pick on her.

GILLIAN: Keith, she's not the issue.

Pause.

KEITH: I see right through you, Toddy. It took Dad a long time dying, didn't it? You must have been driven half crazy by the fact that he took so long. You needed him to die so you can own yourself, prove yourself. You're as ruthless as him.

Pause.

GILLIAN: Keith is right, Todd. You're happy, I can see it in your eyes.

Pause.

TODD: The deal is this. I will buy out Luke's share. Luke, I'll buy your third.

KEITH: Then you'll have two-thirds and therefore a majority share in the company. Luke, think about this.

Silence.

GILLIAN: Luke?

Pause.

LUKE: I did betray the family for Esther. I'd do it again. Because I understood that only by someone being in love with me did I know me—for that brief, fantastic time. And then that monster up there took her away from me. The name Boyce is too much of a burden. I want to be free of that monster. You can have it, Todd. The name, the ghosts. I'm sorry, Keith, I don't know if I could fight the ghosts.

KEITH: Don't let me down, Luke.

GILLIAN: Luke, stand up for something.

Pause.

LUKE: I hate this name.

Silence.

KEITH: [*to* DIANE] You've got it. You won.

TODD: And you, Keith, I can buy you out, too. Just enough money to do it, but I can.

KEITH: You've talked to the bankers about this.

TODD: But I want you to stay on.

KEITH: Go. Stay. What are you on about?

TODD: I admire your attention to detail. You're too much of a handbrake at times, but because I'll be running the company, I'll make the final decisions.

KEITH: You have the nerve to tell your older brother this?

TODD: Just as you had the nerve to treat me like shit. Remember, you made me your driver. Remember? Dad casts me aside, so you employ me as your chauffeur. Your fucking driver! I'd have to wait outside while you wined and dined in restaurants.

KEITH: They were business lunches.

TODD: I'm your brother.

Silence.

KEITH: I'll think about it.

TODD: No. Now.

KEITH: How fucking dare you.

TODD: Now! Or I'll make sure it's years before you get your third. I'll tie it up in the court for years. You can work for me—and I do admire your abilities—or I buy you out.

> *Pause.*

KEITH: Gillian…

GILLIAN: We destroy each other every day, Keith. The last thing I want is for you to say that I gave you the wrong advice.

KEITH: What a good marriage.

DIANE: Why do you two stay together?

LUKE: Mutual hilarity, I suspect.

KEITH: As good a definition as any.

> *Pause.*

GILLIAN: [*to* KEITH] I'm sorry.

KEITH: What are you sorry about?

GILLIAN: [*to* DIANE] I had a very bad miscarriage when we were just married. Ruined my insides. Couldn't and can't have a baby. Dead womb, you see.

KEITH: Gillian… don't say that.

GILLIAN: I did so much want to give him a son.

KEITH: Gillian, stop that.

GILLIAN: Bit of a failure, really. [*Pause.*] I'm so sorry, Keith.

KEITH: Never apologise for that.

> *Pause.*

GILLIAN: The good thing, Diane, is that we never had to agonise over what name we were going to call the kid.

KEITH: Enough, Gillian. Enough…

> *Pause.*

GILLIAN: I will stand by whatever you decide. But you live and breathe this business—remember that.

> *Silence.*

KEITH: The very idea, Todd, of having to kow-tow to you is repulsive to me. I will take my third. Boyce is yours.

Pause.

GILLIAN: Hi-dah-dee. Hi-dah-dah...

Silence.

I think your mother has spent enough time alone. Keith?

KEITH: In a moment...

TODD: Diane...

DIANE: Yes?

TODD: I need to talk to my brothers.

DIANE *is puzzled for a moment and then understands.*

DIANE: Yes. We'd better comfort her. [*To* TODD] I'll tell her that you'll be up soon.

TODD: And could you two pretend civility in front of our mother? Thank you.

The two women exit. TODD *grabs the whisky bottle and starts to pour three drinks.*

KEITH: Never seen you happier, Todd. You're free from Dad. Now all the mistakes are your own. You can't blame anyone else.

Pause.

TODD: Let's not end as enemies.

LUKE: I'm relieved. It's like this obscene burden has been lifted from my shoulders. [*Taking a drink from* TODD] Thank you.

TODD: [*handing a drink to* KEITH] Keith.

KEITH *rejects it.*

Keith, take it.

KEITH *does. Pause.*

What are you thinking, Keith?

Pause.

KEITH: Oh, you know... a fucking million things. But you joining Dad in a coffin right now is on top of the list. [*Pause.*] I'm good at what I do.

TODD: I know that.

KEITH: The business is in my blood.

TODD: Because you're a Boyce. [*Pause.*] You want to stay in?

Pause.

KEITH: Why fucking not. I'll see how long I can stand you.

TODD: I'm pleased. I really am. [*He switches on the Boyce sign.*] It's a good name. A strong name. [*Making a toast*] To us.

ALL: To us.

TODD: And you, Luke?

LUKE: A third of the company is a lot of money and I have every intention of spending it on shagging and drugs or drugs and shagging. Maybe both at the same time.

Pause.

KEITH: Did Dad really say that to you?

TODD: You heard Diane. [*Pause.*] It doesn't matter anymore, does it? [*Pause.*] Best we see Mum. [*Pause.*] Luke? He'll look different dead. He'll be beyond hate. [*Pause.*] I'll tell Mum you'll be up soon.

TODD *exits.* KEITH *finishes his drink.*

KEITH: I think that's why I want to stick around—just to see if he makes it.

KEITH *goes to exit and stops.*

Don't be long.

KEITH *exits.*

LUKE: Once the coffin lid begins to close on you, Daddy, the world will start to forget you. You bullied us. Bullied Mummy. Bullied politicians, terrorised your employees and made this empire. You were a big shot—the Emperor of Sydney. But in a month or so you will be as substantial as a puff of smoke blown away by the wind... and will mean nothing... even to me.

LUKE, *pleased at the thought, goes to the model, turns off the Boyce sign and exits.*

THE END